DO-IT-YOURSELF ENCYCLOPEDIA

A Practical Guide
to Home Improvement,
Repairs and Decorating
containing special material from
The Family Handyman
Do-It-Yourself Encyclopedia
and Family Circle.

Family Circle®

DO-IT-YOURSELF
ENCYCLOPEDIA

VOLUME **1** A-Bar

ROCKVILLE HOUSE PUBLISHERS, INC.
GARDEN CITY, NEW YORK 11530

Acknowledgments

The editors of this series would like to express their thanks and appreciation to the following for their assistance in preparing special sections within this encyclopedia, for their technical advice, and for photographs, art, charts and plans.

Hugh Ackroyd • Alderman Studios • American Plywood Ass'n. • Armstrong Cork Co. • Bakelite Co., Division of Union Carbide and Carbon Corp. • Behr-Manning Corp. • Bicycle Institute of America • Burgess Vibrocrafters, Inc. • California Redwood Ass'n. • Carrier Corp. • Clay Pot Manufacturers Ass'n. • Constad Laboratories • Cummins of John Oster Manufacturing Co. • Reg Van Cuylenberg • Darra-James Co. • Dewalt, Inc. • Dow Chemical Co. • Epoxy Coating Co. • The Formica Company • Alan Hicks • Vincent Lisanti • The Majestic Co., Inc. • Marsh Wall Products, Inc. • Masonite Corp. • Miracle Adhesives • Modernfold Doors, New Castle Products • National Cotton Council • Hans Van Ness • George Nordhausen • Owens-Corning Fiberglas Corp. • P & G Supply Co. • Pittsburgh Plate Glass Co. • Resin Systems • Reynolds Metals Company • O. Philip Roedel • Rubber Flooring Division of the Rubber Manufacturing Assn. • Shellac Information Bureau • Everett Short • Ernest Silva • Skil Corp. • Stanley Tools, Division of the Stanley Works • Structural Clay Products Inst. • Tennessee Eastman Co. • Tile Council of America • Turner Brass Works • United States Plywood Corp. • Wen Products, Inc. • Western Wood Products Ass'n. • Wood Conversion Co. • Woodhill Chemical Co.

Published by arrangement with
The Family Circle, Inc.,
a subsidiary of The New York Times Media Company, Inc.

Publishing Staff

Harold J. Highland *Editorial Director*
E. R. Harris *Executive Editor*
Dorothy Sara *Household Editor*
Frank Rogers *Projects Editor*
E. C. Moore *Staff Photographer*

Consulting Editorial Staff

Ralph Treves *How-To Editor*
Robert B. Stone *Architectural Editor*
William Atlas *Engineering Editor*
Robert F. Hemberger *Heating and Plumbing Editor*
Leon Theil *Industrial Consultant*
Jerome Marcus *Educational Consultant*

Revised Edition

Prepared under the editorial direction of

DICK DEMSKE and L. DONALD MEYERS
with the valued cooperation of

ARTHUR HETTICH Editor of Family Circle
MARGOT L. WOLF Design and Layout
DONALD D. WOLF Production Editor

Abbreviations—Building Terms

The home handyman finds it helpful to know the abbreviations which are commonly used in the building trades. This information is of value when ordering lumber and other materials, reading house plans or project plans and estimates. Here are some of the more widely used abbreviations:

A.C.	alternating current
A.D.	air-dried
av.	average
av. l.	average length
av. w.	average width
bbl.	barrel
bd.	board
bd. ft.	board foot (1 sq. ft. by 1 in. thick)
bdl.	bundle
bev.	beveled
bgs.	bags
B.T.U.	British thermal unit
CL	center line
clg.	ceiling
clr.	clear
C.M.	center matched (tongue - and - groove joints are made along center of the edge)
com.	common
csg.	casing
ctg.	crating
cu. ft.	cubic foot
cu. in.	cubic inch (or cubic inches)
cu. yd.	cubic yard (or cubic yards)
d.	nail size (penny)
D.C.	direct current
D & CM	dressed (1 or 2 sides) and center matched
D & M	dressed and matched (dressed 1 or 2 sides, and tongued - and - grooved on edges. The match may be center or standard.)
D & SM	dressed (1 or 2 sides) and standard matched
D 2S & M	dressed 2 sides and (center or standard) matched
D 2S & SM	dressed 2 sides and standard matched
deg. (or °)	degrees
dia.	diameter
dim.	dimension
D.S.	drop siding
E.	edge
Fahr. (or F.)	Fahrenheit
FAS	firsts and seconds (combined grade of the 2 upper grades of hardwoods)
f. bk.	flat back
facty.	factory (lumber)
F.G.	flat grain
flg.	flooring
f.o.k.	free of knots
frm.	framing
ft. (or ′)	foot (or feet)
gal.	gallon (or gallons)
hdl.	handle (stock)
hdwd.	hardwood
H.P.	horsepower
hrt.	heart
hrtwd.	heartwood
in. (or ″)	inch (or inches)
KD	kiln-dried
k.d.	knocked down
lbr.	lumber
lgth.	length
lin. ft.	linear foot (12 inches)
L.R.	long run
Lr. MCO	long run, mill culls out
manuf.	manufacturer
M.	one thousand
M.b.m.	1000 ft. board measure
M.R.	mill run

M.s.m.	1000 ft. surface measure
m.w.	mixed width
No. or #	number
nt. wt.	net weight
1s & 2s	ones and twos (combined grade of the hardwood grades of firsts and seconds)
ord.	order
oz.	ounce (or ounces)
P.	planed
pat.	pattern
pln.	plain (as in plain sawed)
pn.	partition
qtd.	quartered (referring to hardwoods)
rd.	round
rdm.	random
res.	resawed
rfg.	roofing
rfrs.	roofers
rip.	ripped
r.l.	random length
R.P.M.	revolutions per minute
r.w.	random width
S & E	surfaced 1 side and 1 edge
S 1E	surfaced 1 edge
S1S1E	surfaced 1 side and 1 edge
S1S2E	surfaced 1 side and 2 edges
S 2 E	surfaced 2 edges
S 4 S	surfaced 4 sides
S & CM	surfaced 1 or 2 sides and center matched
S & M	surfaced and matched (surfaced 1 or 2 sides, and tongued-and-grooved on edges. The match may be center or standard.)
S & SM	surfaced 1 or 2 sides and standard matched
S2S & CM	surfaced 2 sides and center matched
S2S & M	surfaced 2 sides and standard or center matched
S2S & SM	surfaced 2 sides and standard matched
sp.	sapwood
SB	standard bead
sd.	seasoned
sdg.	siding
sel.	select
S.E.Sd.	square-edge siding
s.f.	surface feet (an area of 1 sq ft.)
sftwd.	softwood
sh.d.	shipping dry
ship.	shiplap
Sm.	standard matched
s.m.	surface measure
s.n.d.	sap no defect
snd.	sound
sq.	square
sq. E.	square edge
Sq. E & S	square edge and sound
sqrs.	squares
S.S.	single strength
std.	standard
stk.	stock
S.W.	sound wormy
T & G	tongued-and-grooved
TB & S	top, bottom, and sides
tbrs.	timbers
V.G.	vertical grain
w.a.l.	wider, all length
wdr.	wider
wt.	weight
wth.	width
x	multiplied by
yd.	yard (or yards)

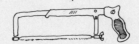

Old hutch with its collection of cookbooks and gardening manuals lends charm and character to this dine-in kitchen. The battered vintage piece was found in a thrift shop, hidden beneath countless coats of paint. Tender-loving care—and lots of sanding—revealed the original wood, which was then stained and waxed.

The real key to success of any finishing or refinishing job is in the preparation and smoothing of the surface.

10

For the heavy jobs, a belt sander is the best bet. This two-speed model includes a detachable dust catcher.

Abrasives

There are many different types of abrasives available to the home handyman today. Most people are familiar with "sandpaper," but steel-wool and mineral blocks also fall within this class. The term "sandpaper," meaning paper coated with abrasive grains, had its birth many years ago, probably when sand was actually used in that way. Today five different mineral grains are used, of various degrees of hardness and toughness, and the term "sandpaper" actually no longer describes the product.

Types of Sandpaper

Coated abrasives are almost the least expensive of the tools in your kit. The slight investment in maintaining a stock of the sizes and types you need, pays off in time saved, greater convenience and better work.

FOR REMOVING OLD PAINT —Flint paper is recommended for the job. There is little advantage in using a harder, sharper abrasive since

SANDING HOW-TO

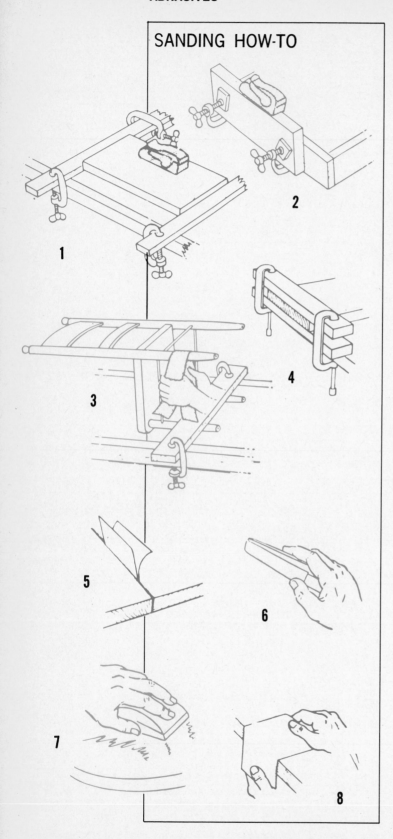

the rapid loading of paint chips dictates the life of the paper. Use coarse grit for first rough sanding and medium grit for the second. Flint paper can be used for final sanding but other papers do a better job.

FOR WOOD—Garnet paper is the preferred choice for hand sanding and finishing wood. It comes in an assortment of grits. The following are the popular grit choices for the various stages of sanding: Very Coarse—1/2; Coarse—0; Medium —2/0; Fine—4/0 and Very Fine— 6/0.

FOR RUST REMOVAL—Emery cloth is usually satisfactory where the job is not too extensive or only a small amount of rust has to be removed. Emery cloth ranks with flint paper as an abrasive for use in those cases where enduring sharpness is not required. If there is an excessive amount of rust, it is best to use a wire

1. To sand a large flat surface, use two strips of wood secured in place with "C" clamps.
2. To sand an edge, set board in a vise or clamp it to the side of an upturned box.
3. To sand chair legs, set chair on a side and "lock" it in place with a board and clamps.
4. To sand end grain, clamp two pieces of wood to top and bottom of board and to work bench.
5. To reduce spots when butting two boards for gluing, slip folded piece of paper between them.
6. To sand a curved surface, use a tapered sanding stick, store-bought or shop-made.
7. Wet sanding is best for primers and between coats when finishing with varnish or enamel.
8. To crease sandpaper, pull with grain up over a sharp corner once or twice as shown.

Sketches courtesy of Behr-Manning Corp.

ABRASIVES AND THEIR USES

TYPE	USE	COLOR	HARDNESS*
Aluminum oxide	hardwood and metals	reddish-brown	9
Crocus	polishing metal to a mirror finish	dull red to purple	2
Emery	on any small, quick sanding job	dull black	8
Flint	. . . . see quartz		
Garnet	softwood and hardwood	red	7
Pumice	final polishing and to cut down (roughen slightly) finishing coats of varnish, etc.	off-white	4
Quartz	to remove old paint and furniture finish	grayish-white	6
Rottenstone	furniture polishing and roughing down varnish and shellac coats	off-white	3
Rouge	polishing of metal	red or green	0
Silicon carbide	fine finishing of wood; also on plastics and metal	gray, green or black	1-10

* The grading of hardness is an indication of the hardness of the abrasive itself and not the grading value of the abrasive paper made of these grains.

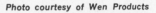

Photo courtesy of Wen Products

Circular sanding discs are handy with an electric drill. The abrasive disc is backed by a rubber pad, giving it flexibility and yet firmness. Keep sander in motion on any surface, especially when using a coarse paper.

There are many types of "flat" sanders the handyman can use; these include the orbital for uniform sanding, straight line for finishing and the reciprocating type, especially useful for smoothing edges of wood pieces.

brush or wire wheel with an electric drill.

FOR POLISHING METAL SURFACES—Crocus cloth will give you a mirror finish on metal parts. It is widely used on gun actions, fishing reels and the like where frictionless smooth movement is essential.

FOR METAL PREPARATION AND FINISHING—Cloth with an aluminum oxide base such as Metal-ite, is best when preparing metal for

SELECTING THE RIGHT ABRASIVE FOR THE JOB

MATERIAL	ABRASIVE	ROUGH	SANDING MEDIUM	FINE
Aluminum	Aluminum oxide	40	80	100
Brass	Silicon carbide	40	80	120
Composition board	Garnet	1	½	0
Copper	Aluminum oxide	40	80	120
Cork	Garnet	3	1	0
Glass	Silicon carbide	50	120	320
Hardwood	Aluminum oxide or garnet	2½	½	3/0
Iron	Silicon carbide	30	60	100
Paint (removal)	Flint	2	½	. . .
Softwood	Garnet	1½	0	2/0
Steel	Aluminum oxide	30	60	100

Note: Grit is the designation of the number of grains which, when set end to end, equals one inch, as 120, 320. Numbers like ½ and 1 are arbitrary designations.

GUIDE TO ABRASIVE BELT SELECTION

TYPE OF WOOD	ROUGH	FINISH	FINE FINISH
Birch	2½—1	½—0	2/0—4/0
Cypress	2½—1½	½—0	2/0
Fir	1½—1	½—0	2/0
Gum	2½—1½	½—0	2/0—3/0
Mahogany	2½—1½	½—0	2/0—3/0
Maple	2½—1	½—0	2/0—4/0
Maple (curly)	2½—1½	½—0	2/0—4/0
Oak	2½—1½	½—0	2/0—4/0
Walnut	2½—1½	½—0	2/0—4/0
White pine	1½—1	0	2/0
Yellow pine	2 —1½	½	0

14

Courtesy of Porter Cable, Inc.

a paint or lacquer finish. It is available in sheets, discs, rolls and other convenient forms for use.

FOR HARDWOODS AND METALS—Paper and cloth such as Adalox offer the handyman a sharp, hard and enduring abrasive for finishing. It is particularly good with power sanders and can also be used for hand sanding operations. Because of its long cutting life, the sanding is seldom interrupted for renewing this type of abrasive.

FOR PLASTICS, COMPOSITION MATERIALS AND METALS—Durite paper, coated with diamond-hard silicon carbide grit, is exceptionally sharp. In its waterproof form, it is most valuable for wet sanding primers and undercoats for enamel, lacquer and other surfacing materials.

FOR FLOOR FINISHING — Special grit paper is available for floor sanding machines, which are often available on a rental basis from the local hardware store. For old floors, start by sanding with Very Coarse or Coarse paper, 3½ or 4 grit. Follow this with a Fine paper, ½ and give the floors a final sanding with Very Fine floor sanding paper, 2/0. On the other hand, with new floors, either softwood or hardwood, start with Medium grit paper, 2½ and then use Fine, ½, finishing with Very Fine floor paper.

Sanding Techniques

The first step in reducing sanding effort is to select the right coated abrasive for the job. That is, the one which will cut sharpest and fastest.

The second step is to hold the work steady. This may seem like an obvious requirement, but it is too

Plenty of working space makes any sanding job easier, while adequate ventilation is a must.

often neglected. Note the accompanying sketches for a few suggestions for doing this job. Do not hold the work in one hand and sand with the other; it is best to avoid muscular fatigue before you start.

Always use a backing surface for the abrasive paper when sanding. Use a sanding block, even a convenient piece of wood, or a power sander; never just your hand.

When using a power sander, cut the abrasive paper or cloth to the proper size so that it covers the entire sanding pad.

15

Accident Prevention

Safety first is the rule for all members of the family, in and around the house. Safety is no accident! It is the practice of common sense, following certain basic rules and eliminating or minimizing hazards. It is especially essential for the do-it-yourself handyman to follow safety rules. No job should be undertaken without full knowledge of what must be done, the right tools needed for the job and awareness of possible hazards.

It is essential to understand what causes accidents if you are to be successful in preventing them. Never do any do-it-yourself project unless you are fully awake and alert. Fatigue increases your reaction time, and in that split second, you may have an accident.

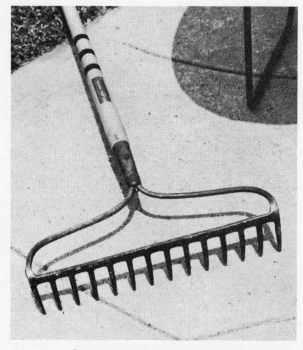

16

Put your garden tools away as soon as you're finished. If these must be around, keep the sharp, cutting edges facing the ground.

Electrical Hazards

Wherever electrical appliances, lighting fixtures, wiring and outlets are located, indoors or outdoors, caution must be exercised in testing, repairing or replacing them.

Faulty house wiring, broken or frayed cords, damaged sockets and switches are dangerous. If you have any doubts about their efficiency and safety, replace them at once!

Never undertake any electrical repair in the house without first shutting off the electrical current. If you know which fuse controls the line on which you plan to work, remove that fuse. Take it out of the fuse box; just don't unscrew it part of the way. It is best to put the fuse away, somewhere removed from the fuse box and to hang a note on the fuse box to warn anyone that electrical work is being done and not to put a fuse in on the line. If you don't know which fuse controls the line, pull the master switch and shut off all the current.

Fires often occur through overheating of wires which are carrying too much current or because of an electric arc in the presence of combustible material. Therefore do not use too many appliances on any one line or plug them into one outlet by using a multiple extension cord.

Remember: the blowing of a fuse is a sign—a warning that your circuit is carrying too much current. It may only be a temporary overload, but even a momentary overload is sufficient to blow a fuse. If your fuse blows, play it safe—examine the load the line is carrying.

D o   n o t   purchase appliances marked "A.C. only" if the current in your house is D.C.; in that case, you

Even a well-planned workshop such as this one, is not a safe place to work unless properly laid out for easy access. Good lighting is another necessity. Be sure all outlets used to power your tools are adequately grounded and protected by fuses or circuit breakers.

can buy either D.C. or A.C. and D.C. appliances. A motor (by itself or in an appliance) that works on both A.C. and D.C. is called a universal motor. Look at the label of approval of the Board of Underwriters' Laboratories, before buying, to be sure that it is a safe appliance for your home.

If your hands are wet, don't touch any appliance. The same goes if you're standing on a wet spot. This is especially true in the bathroom, kitchen or laundry room. All handles on an appliance should be covered with insulating material (generally plastic) and not left as an exposed metal part.

Do not answer the telephone unless your hands are dry. It may look glamourous to see a movie where the telephone is in the bathroom, but in actual practice, this constitutes an electrical hazard.

Don't use long cords all around the room. Add extra outlets if you need them. Cords stretched around the room are potential fire hazards, particularly dangerous if run under a carpet or rug. The long wires are also dangerous for toddlers.

If you use a portable extension cord with a light attached to it, whether it be in the garage or basement or in the workshop, keep the light away from anything combustible, like paper or a thin curtain. A wire "cage" should always be used around the bulb, for accident prevention.

Fire Hazards

Rubbish, waste paper and other combustible materials should not be collected near the house. They should be kept in safe covered metal receptacles and burned before any large amount accumulates.

Bonfires, too, are hazards and should not be left to "burn out by themselves" but must be watched until the very end. It is best not to burn rubbish or have a bonfire any closer to the house than fifty feet. Dried

17

DO

Rags which contain grease, oil or paint must not be kept around. If left unprotected, they present a fire hazard. Always clean up after you have painted and dispose of all paint-soaked rags. If you must store them, keep them in a tightly closed container. A mason jar is exceedingly handy for such purposes. It has a tightly-sealed screwcap cover. Because it's made of glass, you can easily see what's stored inside. But because it's made of glass, it's easily breakable. Keep such jars away from shelf edges and other locations where there is danger of breakage. If you use metal containers with tight covers for such storage, label the contents on the outside of the can.

DON'T

grass, too, must not be left to accumulate. As it dries, it generates heat and can ignite. If you cannot dispose of dried grass in any other way, burn it.

Some plastics, celluloid and all other similar materials as well as photographic films are highly combustible. Be cautious about smoking, lighting matches or having these materials near an open fire or fireplace.

Basements and attics are rubbish-accumulating centers and are to be considered danger spots where fire is concerned. Give these extra rooms or storage spots periodic check-ups and clear out all non-essential materials.

Chimneys, flues, fireplaces and smokepipes must be cleaned regularly in order to remove the accumu-

lated soot. Defective chimneys and flues are causes of unnecessary fires in the home. Any defects or damages should be repaired instantly.

A close-meshed wire or fire screen should always be kept in front of the fireplace. It is best to avoid combustible flooring next to the fireplace; instead, have the floor near the fireplace made of tiles, stone or brick. Also avoid throwing excelsior or large quantities of paper or other flammable materials into the fireplace to burn; it's too exposed for safety in the home.

Portable hand fire-extinguishers are available for use in and around the home. When buying such items, be certain that they bear the seal of approval of the Board of Underwriters' Laboratories.

If you have no extinguisher available and a fire breaks out, call the Fire Department or Police Department at once. Get everyone out of the house. It is more important to save a life than to try to rescue some material possessions.

The prompt application of water or the use of blankets thrown over the blaze may be effective in extinguishing a small fire before it has a chance to grow into something disasterous. Use a pail, partially filled with water. Or even a broom soaked in water may often be used with good results to beat out a small blaze. A garden hose is, of course, an excellent fire-fighter to have on hand. There are fog nozzles, easily attached to the hose, to combat home fire.

Ladder Safety

Although no actual statistics are available, accidents involving ladders rate high. A good ladder is one of the most useful accessories for the handyman, but it must be used properly. Safety is important whether you are a housewife using a small stepladder in the kitchen or you are a home handyman using a 30′ extension ladder outside the house to paint the trim.

Whether using a ladder indoors or outdoors, you can avoid accidents by observing a few simple rules.

1. While aluminum or magnesium ladders are easier to handle than wood ones, remember that metal is a conductor of electricity. It is important to keep a metal ladder from coming into contact with electric power lines.

2. Don't paint the ladder; the color will keep you from noticing such defects as cracks or splits.

3. The safest angle for a ladder is to place the feet of the ladder about a quarter of its length away from the wall. For example, a 15-foot ladder should be set away (on its feet) about 4 feet from the wall.

4. Make certain that the ladder is on firm ground and won't slip. If you use a metal ladder and rest it on concrete walk or driveway, use rubber-bottom safety feet with the ladder. If you use a wood ladder, it should have rubber "feet" permanently attached to the bottom of it.

5. Make sure that the top of the

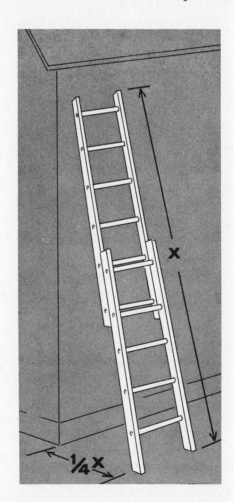

The foot of an extension ladder should be set away from the wall a distance equal to one-fourth the ladder height.

19

ladder, against the wall, is also braced properly and not on a surface where it will slide. Don't put the top of a ladder so that it rests against a screen or window pane.

6. A ladder on a roof must be thoroughly secured, and for this purpose you can obtain roof hooks to attach to the ladder at any hardware store.

7. Don't set your ladder up so that it is directly in front of a door. If that position is necessary, lock the door and put a warning sign on it. It is a better idea to have someone stand by to make certain that the door is not inadvertently opened.

8. Never climb an extension ladder or any long ladder on a very windy day. If you must use the ladder then, have someone hold the base of the ladder as you climb up, stay up there and work and when you climb down again afterwards.

9. An easy way to carry a ladder is to paint a strip at the center of it, then take hold of the ladder and you'll have an even balance.

10. When climbing a ladder, face the ladder, going up and coming down, and take one step at a time.

11. If you're working high up, don't go any higher than the third rung from the top of the ladder and always wear skid-proof soled shoes. If you're using a step ladder, do not stand on the top step; the highest you should go is the second step from the top on a tall stepladder, over 3 feet, or next to the top on shorter ladders.

12. A chore which needs both hands, such as hanging storm sash or screens, must be figured out beforehand, so that you don't teeter on the ladder with your hands holding heavy or swaying objects. Have someone pass them up to you, or perhaps you can pull them up with a rope.

13. If you need both hands for a quick job, grab hold of a rung of the ladder with your leg, or perhaps pass your elbow through a convenient rung.

14. Don't try to reach over too far, when on a ladder. It's best to get off and to move the ladder the few inches. Don't hold a paint can when you're on the ladder; provide a hook on which to hang the can.

15. If you own an extension ladder, and want to raise or lower it, brace the base of the ladder (on the ground) against your foot, and holding on to the ladder, lift it away from the house with one hand until it is almost vertical. Holding it with one hand, use the other hand to pull the rope which extends the ladder.

16. Furthermore, check the rope on your extension ladder periodically to see that there are no weak spots.

Stairways

Whether outdoor or indoor stairways, they must be kept clear of toys, bundles, rubbish. Tripping on stairs is one of the most common household accidents.

Dark stairways leading to an attic or a basement should be adequately lighted with a switch placed at the bottom and at the top of the stairway to control the light. The bottom and top stairs should be painted, preferably yellow as mentioned in the **Color** section, or in some other light color. If you do not wish to paint the entire step, paint a narrow band, about 1″ wide, along the outer edge.

A handrail or banister must be provided on all stairways, especially those leading to porches outdoors because of the danger in wet or icy weather.

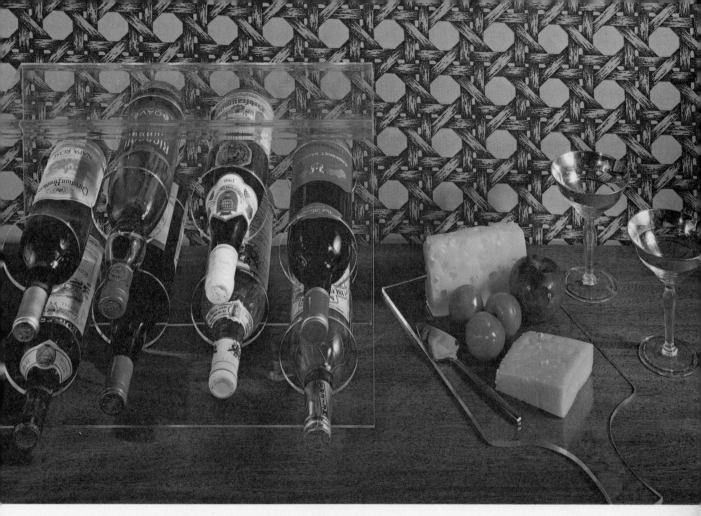

Wine rack and cutting board are of acrylic.

Acrylic Plastics

One of the newer do-it-yourself materials is acrylic plastic. It has a multitude of uses in decorating and construction. Not only is it attractive, but it is also about 17 times more breakage-resistant than untempered glass. For this reason, it is often used in place of glass in hazardous locations such as storm doors. Its most popular use, as the pictures on this page attest, is for decorating.

Working with Acrylics

The material is fairly easy for the do-it-yourselfer to work with. Leave protective paper in place when cutting. To scribe and break acrylic plastic, place the point of a special "cutting tool" or similar scribing tool at the edge of the material and, applying firm pressure, draw the tool the full length of the material. Do this five or six times for thicknesses from .100-inch to .187-inch, and seven to ten times for ¼-inch.

The scribed line should then be positioned face up over a ¾-inch-diameter dowel running the length of the intended break. To break, hold the larger side of the sheet with one hand and apply downward pressure on the short side of the break with the other hand. The hands should be kept adjacent to one another and successively repositioned about two inches in back of the break as it progresses along the scribed line. The minimum cut-off width is 1½ inches.

Cutting with Power Saws

Do *not* remove protective masking paper before cutting. If cutting unmasked sheet is unavoidable, apply masking tape on both sides of the intended cut to reduce friction and gumming behind the blade.

Saber and jig saw blades should have at least 14 teeth per inch for cutting acrylic plastic, and band saw blades should have 10 teeth or more per inch. For straight cuts, clamp a straight edge to the material and guide the tool along the edge. Hold the material down firmly when cutting and do not force feed.

When using a circular saw, a plywood-type blade is best, and blade height should be just a little more than thickness of the sheet. Do not force feed.

Drilling

Either hand or electric drills may be used on acrylic plastic. Use standard metal twist drills or purchase a special bit for electric drills from your dealer. Back the material with soft wood, and clamp or hold firmly. Use very slow speed with hand drill, but use the highest speed available for electric drills. Do not force feed either type of drill.

Be especially careful when point of drill is penetrating other side of material. Slow electric drill down as much as possible at that point.

Acrylic plastic is scored with a special scribing tool available at dealer's. Keep masking paper on material until scoring and breaking process is completed.

After material has been scored from five to ten times (see text), it is placed over ¾-inch dowel and broken. If material is over ¼-inch thick, use a power saw.

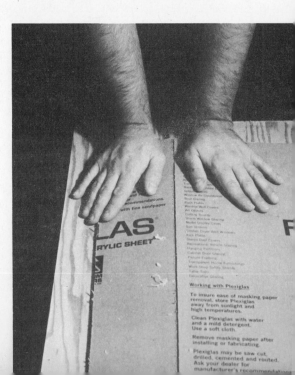

Edge Finishing

Sawed edges and other tool marks should be removed by scraping the edge with a sharp knife, then filing with a fine-tooth metal file and/or sanding with medium grit paper. This will insure maximum breakage resistance. To further improve the appearance of the surface or edge, follow the initial finishing with "wet or dry" grit sandpaper. For a transparent edge, follow this step with very fine grits, then buff with a clean muslin wheel dressed with a good grade of fine-grit buffing compound. Finish up with a clean, soft-flannel wheel.

Cementing

Capillary cementing with a solvent (methylene chloride "MDC" or ethylene dichloride "EDC" or 1-1-2 trichlorethane) is an easy method of joining two pieces of acrylic plastic. Sand surfaces to be cemented but do not polish.

Remove protective masking paper. Hold pieces together with strips of masking tape. Apply solvent with a

Sawed edges and other tool marks are removed from acrylic plastic by scraping the edges smooth with a sharp knife or by sanding with medium grit (60-80) paper.

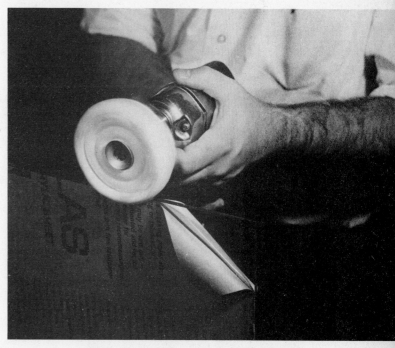

For a transparent edge, follow 60-80 grit sanding with "wet or dry" 150-grit sanding and final 400-grit finish. Buff with a clean muslin wheel and fine-grit compound.

Circular saws are ideal for straight cuts. Use a plywood-type blade, with at least six teeth per inch. Set blade height just a little above the sheet. Do not force.

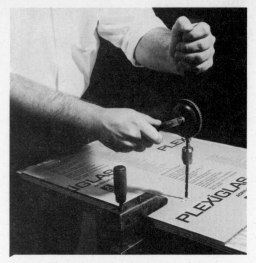

Acrylic plastic can be worked with an electric drill using a special bit. Back material with soft wood, clamped or held firmly. Use highest speed available.

When using a hand drill, standard twist drills commonly used for metals are recommended. Back with wood and hold firmly. When hand drilling, use very slow speed.

Pieces of plastic can be joined together with a solvent using capillary action. Surfaces to be joined should be sanded but not polished to make most lasting bond.

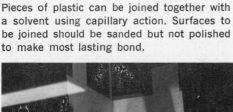

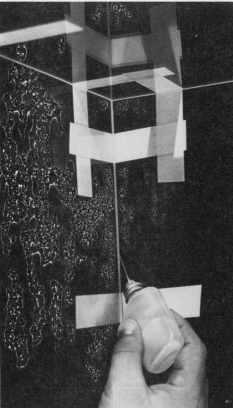

Acrylic plastic can be painted, scribed, textured or decorated with materials such as paper, cloth or foil. Best material for decorating is that which has pressure-sensitive backing, but others can be applied with either spray-on adhesives applied to both surfaces or clear lacquer sprayed on the plastic. When painting, use lacquer, enamel or oil paints. When used outdoors, "Krylon" provides weatherability.

Desk top, floor protector, hobby case, lamp, pencil holder, poster cover, shadow box—all are plastic.

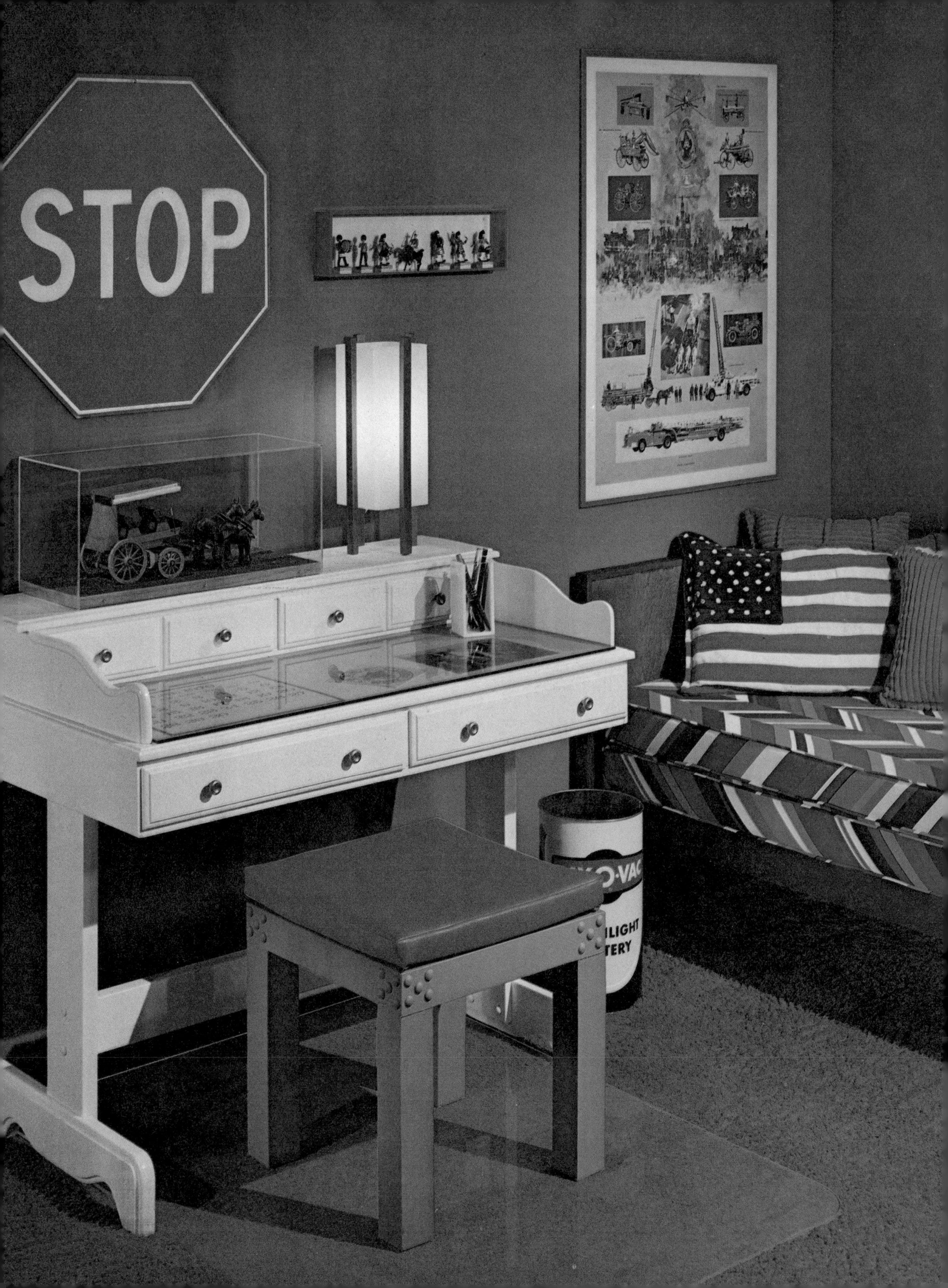
STOP

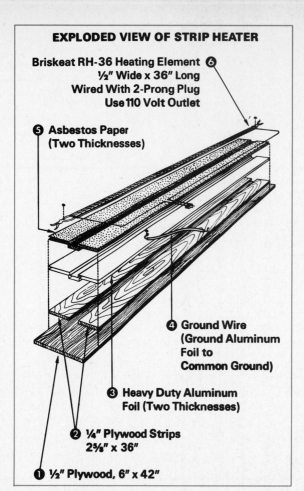

EXPLODED VIEW OF STRIP HEATER

Briskeat RH-36 Heating Element ❻
½" Wide x 36" Long
Wired With 2-Prong Plug
Use 110 Volt Outlet

❺ Asbestos Paper
(Two Thicknesses)

❹ Ground Wire
(Ground Aluminum
Foil to
Common Ground)

❸ Heavy Duty Aluminum
Foil (Two Thicknesses)

❷ ¼" Plywood Strips
2⅝" x 36"

❶ ½" Plywood, 6" x 42"

Make your own strip heater for straight bending. Heating element, available at most Plexiglass dealers, uses 110 volts.

"solvent applicator" available at most dealers, or use syringe, fine-spout oil can, eye dropper or very small paint brush. Let joint dry thoroughly.

Use contact cement or household adhesives to attach acrylic plastic to other materials—or vice versa.

Caution: Solvents may be toxic if inhaled for extended periods of time or if swallowed. Many are also inflammable. Use in a well-ventilated area and keep away from children.

Strip Heat Forming

Acrylic plastic sheet can be formed along a straight line by strip heating.

Remove the protective masking paper. Place sheet on supporting frame of strip heater (buy one at dealer's or make your own—see illustration) with the area to be formed directly above the heating element. Do not let the sheet touch the heating element itself.

Material should not be heated to a temperature higher than 340 degrees F. Surface overheating will cause scorching and bubbling. If this does occur, increase the distance between the heating element and the plastic sheet. Allow the material to heat until it softens or melts in the area to be formed. Bend gently to the desired angle, keeping heated side of material on the outside of the bend. Hold firmly until cool.

Be sure material is heated thoroughly before bending. Otherwise, stress crazing (small internal fractures) will result. Practice on scrap material first. Do not attempt to bend material over ¼-inch thick.

Caution: Do not leave strip heater unattended, and work in well-ventilated room.

How to install an air-conditioner without completely spoiling the view? Surround the unit with see-through acrylic plastic.

A roomful of projects that the do-it-yourselfer can make of acrylic plastics: room divider, tables, lamp.

Handsome sideboard of acrylic plastic is flanked by shelves of lacquered wood.

Addition to Your House

Addition for a One-Story House

If you are like millions of other American families, you have outgrown your home. That's what happened to the family whose children are playing in the yard on the preceding pages. Their solution was to design a new addition.

Using the ingenious Add-a-Room Design System developed by the ar-

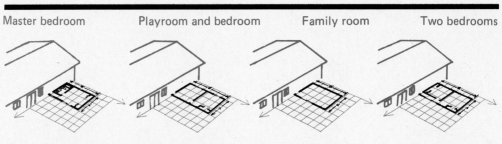

Master bedroom   Playroom and bedroom   Family room   Two bedrooms

Floor plans that can be worked out with the system.

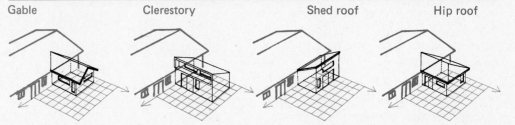

Gable   Clerestory   Shed roof   Hip roof

A choice of roof styles for your type of house.

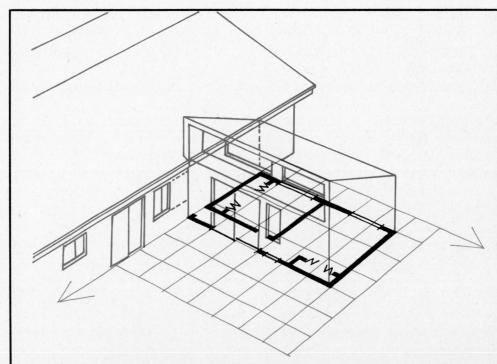

Plan of a two-bedroom addition.

chitectural firm of Hobbs-Fukui Associates with the cooperation of the American Plywood Association, the family came up with a two-bedroom extension at the rear of their home. The system gives a set of guidelines with unlimited design possibilities. It allows plenty of flexibility and includes architectural options so that it can be used for just about any style of home—modern or traditional, one-story or two-story. Following the guidelines, you can (as this family did) design an addition specifically tailored to your specific needs—master bedroom, playroom, family room. In this case, the shell of the addition was built by a local contractor and the family then finished the inside themselves. Thus, the savings in both architectural and building costs were considerable. If you are considering expanding your house to match your family's growth, study this case history.

The First Steps

The very first step was to check with the local building authorities to see if there were any restrictions and zoning codes that would prevent them from adding on. They found they could build to the rear, but not the sides or front—something you should look into in addition to building permits and the like.

The family knew that they needed two bedrooms, so it was logical their new addition be built near the existing bedroom area of their home. There was a window in the wall of one bedroom where a door could be cut without disturbing a large wall area. This is the spot where they decided to make the connection. (The function of your addition is

important. If it's a family room you want, consider adding on to the kitchen. A den might be placed off the living room area, a work room off the garage.)

How Big?

The family decided that an overall 12 × 24-foot addition would be best for their two bedrooms. Working with tracing paper placed over a worksheet laid out on a 4-foot grid, the family refined their ideas for a floor plan. Using the guidelines of the design system, they plotted out the existing wall of their home on the grid. Then they transferred the final floor plan of the addition to see how the twain should meet. (For economy and ease of construction, you should work with 4-foot dimensions.)

Since the house is a one-story contemporary, they felt a clerestory roof would be the most interesting for their addition. They drew this roof style on their worksheet. Before any work was done at all, they had a good idea of what the finished product would look like. (The style of the existing house is of primary importance here. Options of the system include gable, shed and hip roofs that can be used for one-story as well as two-story houses.)

Working with the guidelines of the system, the family chose two small bedroom windows for privacy at the rear of the addition. They also added a 6-foot sliding glass door to create a patio entrance. They selected windows, doors, roofing and plywood siding materials that were similar to those of their existing house. (Your choice here is unlimited and depends entirely on the function of your addition. However, it's best to blend

31

your addition with the existing house to keep it from standing out like a sore thumb.)

Addition for a Two-Story House

Another family, living in a two-story house, found they needed a family-room addition. Using the same Add-A-Room Design System, they reviewed all the alternatives open to them. After checking with the building authorities and studying the existing house, the most logical place for the addition was to the rear and off a small dining area near the kitchen.

Working with tracing paper on the worksheet, they planned the 16 × 24-foot addition in the same manner as the other family did. Since this house is two stories and more traditional in feeling, a gable roof was chosen. Similar materials were used

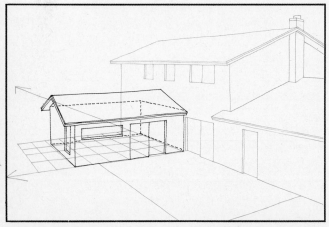

for the addition. A sliding glass door was installed at one side to open out to the existing patio. Materials for both houses will vary in cost from $4.50 to $6 per square foot, depending on the design you choose and the part of the country where you live.

If you would like more information on the Add-A-Room Design System, write to the American Plywood Association, Dept. 650, P.O. Box 2277, Tacoma, Wash. 98401.

Adhesives

There's a lot more to using an adhesive than merely applying it to the surface of the pieces to be joined. With the proper adhesive you can get a bonding that is stronger than the material itself.

Before proceeding, it should be noted that there are many different types of adhesives. Some are designed to do a specialized job while others can be used for several purposes. Some adhesives or glues bond instantly and require no clamping while others set more slowly and the work must be clamped until the adhesive is thoroughly dry.

There are adhesives for bonding any one material to any other material. They bond in two ways. Either the adhesive enters the pores of the material; this is technically known as mechanical adhesion. On the other hand, the adhesive may stay on the surface of a non-porous material; this is known as surface tension adhesion.

Adhesives and Their Uses

Casein glue—This is one of the few glues you can use in a cold workshop, even on rough wood and poorly fitted joints. It comes in powder form

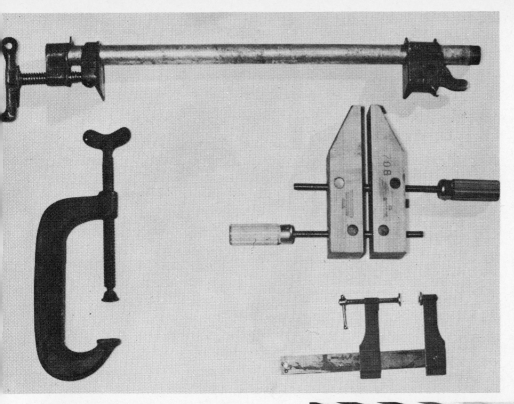

There are many different types of clamps which the home handyman can use to hold the work while the adhesive is drying. Here are a few of the more commonly used clamps which you can find in most handyman workshops: (clockwise, starting at the top) pipe clamp, hand screw, small bar clamp and a large C-clamp. Each has a specific purpose when used with adhesives in the workshop.

and is mixed with cold water, usually 1 part adhesive to 2 parts water (by weight). For best results, leave mixture stand for about 15 minutes and then stir again and apply. It's safe to use at any temperature above freezing and only moderate clamping pressure is necessary. Here's a time guide—hardwoods take at least 5 hours and softwoods about 3 hours for the adhesive to set when clamps are used.

Casein, flexible latex—Here's one to bond really difficult-to-glue materials. It can be used to join metal and other non-porous materials to wood and other porous and semiporous materials to each other.

Cellulose cement—This is a fast drying, transparent adhesive that is best suited for small repair work, such as china mending, or for model building. It comes already prepared,

Always protect the face or surface of the wood from the metal edge of the clamp. As you apply pressure the metal will "eat" into the wood if you don't use a protective block.

33

generally in a tube for instant application.

Epoxy—A product of modern science, this material is capable of pro-

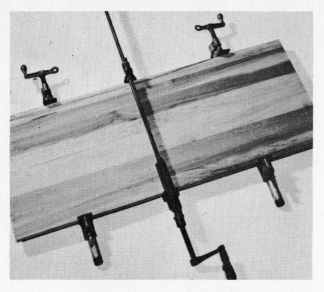

Alternate pipe or bar clamps when you glue boards edge of edge. Remember to sand the edges between boards perfectly smooth before applying the adhesive and adding the clamps.

ducing bonds of fantastic strength. It can be used to fasten any two materials. Because it is quite costly, however, it is not often used in large amounts but is ideal for repairs where a small dab will do. Packaged in squeeze tubes by many manufacturers. Most epoxies have two components—a resin and a hardener—in separate tubes. They are not mixed until ready to proceed because they have a limited pot life. Setting time can range from an hour to a full day.

Hot hide glue—Although not generally used by home handymen today for gluing about the house, it is an old adhesive that still does an excellent job. You can buy hide glue in cake, flake or ground forms. Soak the glue in lukewarm water overnight—1 part glue to 2 parts water, by weight or according to the maker's instructions. Use glass ovenware or metal containers double-boiler fashion to keep it below 150° F, and apply hot. Heat only the quantity

"C" clamp pliers are likewise very useful in place of the ordinary "C" clamp. A mere twist of the set screw on the edge of the handle make the clamp jaws larger or smaller.

Ordinary rope will do the trick when it's necessary to clamp chair legs while glue is setting. Take up on the rope slack by twisting in a small stick; tie securely.

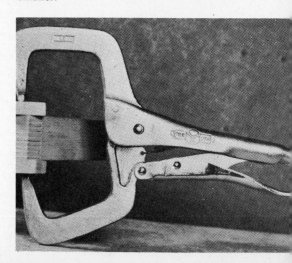

needed; frequent reheating weakens the glue. It sets fast, but requires tight clamping and matched joints for proper bonding.

Liquid fish glue—It is convenient to use as it comes already mixed in liquid form. If, however, it's too thick, you can "thin" it by setting the jar in a pan of hot water; but don't boil! After applying the adhesive to the pieces to be joined, wait for about 5 to 10 minutes before closing the joint. Clamp the work and let it stay undisturbed for at least 24 hours.

Liquid hide glue—Stronger than wood, this glue is fast setting and can be used anywhere so long as the temperature is higher than 60 degrees. In many ways it's similar to hot glue, but is more foolproof. It can be used for a wide variety of work.

Resorcinol resin—A room-temperature setting adhesive, works well indoors and out, in hot or cold. Joints with this type of adhesive are very durable. Leaving the work under clamps for about 8 hours will produce a long-lasting joint. This adhesive is sold as a thick liquid with a separate powered catalyst, which are mixed together just prior to using.

Synthetic rubber and resin—There are several different classes of adhesives in this group. There is the instant bonding group that joins two pieces when only moderate pressure is applied for only a few moments. Furthermore, there is the sensitive structural type, which requires a minimum of clamping. Finally, there is a general purpose thermoplastic type made of synthetic rubber and resin.

The instant type is used basically for bonding plastic laminated surfaces, such as Formica, Micarta, Consoweld. The general purpose combination is highly versatile; it can be used not only to join like materials, but also to join one type with another, including: metal, wood,

If you have no clamps, you can make your own bar clamps by using wood wedges. Nail or screw a block of wood at each side leaving sufficient space to drive a double wedge.

Vise clamps, generally used to hold pieces of wood for nailing, are exceptionally useful as gluing clamps. By using this type of clamp, you are assured of a perfectly square joint.

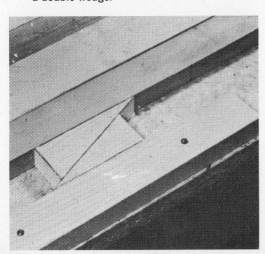

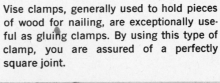

35

Type of Glue
Liquid Hide and Fish Glue
Brands include LePage's Liquid Glue, Franklin Liquid Glue and Rogers Isenglass.

Good for
Furniture and cabinetwork, general wood gluing.

Not Good for
Outdoor furniture and anything exposed to dampness.

Advantages
Strong, easy to use, light color, fills cracks and gaps in joints, resists heat, mold.

Disadvantages
It is not water resistant, must be warmed if used in a cold location or in cold weather.

Type of Glue
Powdered Casein
Brands include Casco LePage's Casein Glue.

Good for
General woodworking, especially oily woods: teak, yew, lemon.

Not Good for
Acid woods unless staining is not important; outdoor furniture.

Advantages
Strong, fairly water resistant, works in cool locations, fills cracks and poor joints.

Disadvantages
Must be mixed 15 minutes before using, subject to mold, stains dark woods.

Type of Glue
Resorcinol
Brands include Cascophen, U.S. Plywood Phenol Resorcinol Glue.

Good for
Outdoor furniture, boats, items that may be soaked.

Not Good for
Work done where the temperature is below 70°.

Advantages
Very strong, waterproof, works well with poor joints.

Disadvantages
Powder and catalyst must be carefully mixed, has dark color.

ADVANTAGES AND DISADVANTAGES OF VARIOUS GLUES

Type of Glue
White Polyvinyl
Brands include Cascorez, Wilhold, Presto-Set Glue, Elmer's Glue-all, LePage's Sure-Grip White Glue.

Good for
Model work, paper, leather, small wood assemblies, mending.

Not Good for
Anything requiring resistance to stress and water.

Advantages
Always ready to use at any temperature, non-staining.

Disadvantages
Has high cold-flow after setting; good only for light work.

Type of Glue
Plastic Resin
Brands include Weldwood, Cascamite, Formica Urea Resin Glue, LePage's Plastic Resin Glue.

Good for
Furniture, veneering, work exposed to dampness.

Not Good for
Oily woods or poorly fitted joints when clamps are not used.

Advantages
Very strong, waterproof, leaves light-colored joint.

Disadvantages
Must be mixed for each use, needs heavy clamp pressure.

Type of Glue
Flake Animal
Brands include Craftsman Hide Glue.

Good for
Quantity woodworking, furniture.

Not Good for
Anything that may be used or stored in damp places.

Advantages
Light-colored joints that need no bleaching, fills cracks and gaps in the wood.

Disadvantages
Inconvenient for quick or occasional use, must be kept hot.

plastic, fabric, ceramic, rubber, leather, plaster, glass, cement, etc.

Urea resin—Available in powder form, this type of adhesive is mixed with cold water, generally 10 parts glue to 6 parts water. Unlike casein glue, this adhesive can be used as soon as it's mixed. However, once mixed, it should not be kept for more than 6 to 7 hours. Workroom, wood glue and curing temperature should be 70° F or higher. Well fitted joints and high clamping pressure are required.

White polyvinyl liquid glue—Relatively new in the adhesives family, this type has become exceedingly popular because of its convenience, speed in setting, and stain-proof quality. Available in both squeeze tube and bottle, this adhesive dries transparent and sets within a half hour. Very little clamping pressure is needed. This is a fine many-purpose adhesive, but is not moistureproof or heat resistant although different brands may vary to some extent in this respect.

1. If you use a powdered glue, measure it carefully if you want strong joints. There is a correct amount of water or catalyst for each powdered glue. Don't guess at the proportions. If you use flake glue, mix each ounce with 1½ ounces of water, let stand overnight and then use hot.

2. Watch the temperature when you use the glue. Animal glues won't spread when cold, and plastic-resin glues won't set properly when the temperature is below 70°. For best results with all glues, have both the glue and the work at 70° or higher.

3. Make it fit properly! No glue produces a strong joint when the fit is poor. Where you must glue a poorly fitted joint, as in repairing a loose chair rung, use an animal, casein or resorcinol glue, if possible.

How To Glue Wood

When a glue joint fails, there's a reason. But post-mortems are no substitute for durability. Check your own

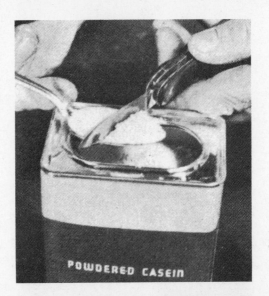

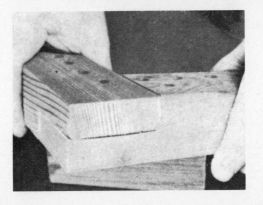

4. Clean old work thoroughly! When regluing a broken joint, scrape or sandpaper the old surface down to bare wood. Most glues work by penetrating the porous wood grain; they cannot get a grip on surfaces sealed by old glue or paint.

5. Clamp the work properly after the glue is applied. The clamp is too tight, forcing most of the glue out of the joint, and there are no blocks to spread the pressure and protect the work being glued.

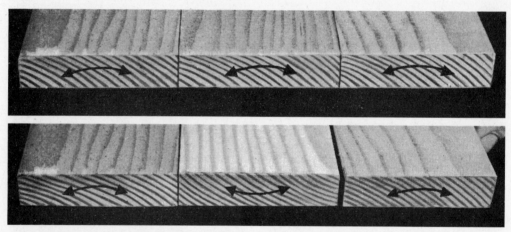

6. When gluing several boards together, alternate the grain. If you glue stock edge to edge—when making a tabletop, for example—lay out the boards so that the direction of the grain alternates, presenting the heartwood side of the grain up on every other board. In the upper section of the photograph, all grain curves downward, increasing the chances that finished piece will bow later. In the lower section of the photograph, the center piece is turned with the heartwood side up, canceling out the tendency for finished piece to cup in one direction.

38

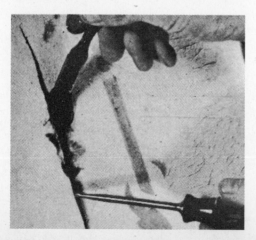

7. Apply the glue properly! Don't wear the glue brush to a frazzle using it in the wrong place, such as filling a crack. There are better ways of putting the glue where you want it. An old saw blade or even a windshield wiper does a fast job of covering broad surfaces.

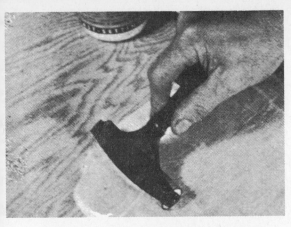

8. An old photo-print roller, if you're a camera bug, can be used to spread an even layer of glue on a plywood panel, if you don't have a notched spreader or an old saw blade.

9. Chair rungs or other similar joints can be reglued without pulling them apart if a small hole is drilled into the dowel hole and the glue pumped into it with an oil can. A hypodermic needle will shoot small quantities of glue under blistered veneer or a paint-striping tool will spread it in narrow ribbons for grooves, inlay borders, cracks and other long thin work.

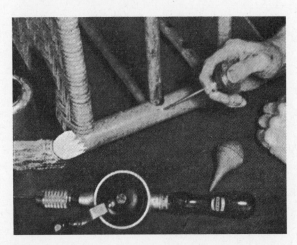

GLUING PROCEDURE AT A GLANCE

Type of Glue	How To Prepare	How To Apply	Minimum Room Temperature	Setting Time at 70° Softwood—Hardwood	
Liquid animal or fish	If room is cold, warm glue to 70° or higher.	Spread on both surfaces; let get tacky before joining.	Sets best above 70° but can be used in colder room if glue is warmed.	12 hours	24 hours
Casein	Mix equal parts of glue and water. Let stand 10 minutes and stir again.	Use within 8 hours after mixing; put on a thick coat.	Any temperature above freezing, but the warmer the better.	2 hours	4 hours
Polyvinyl	Comes ready to use.	Spread on and clamp at once.	Any temperature above freezing; sets faster if warmed.	20 minutes	30 minutes
Plastic resin	Mix 2 parts of powder with ½ to 1 part of water.	Apply thin coat to one surface only.	Must be 70° or warmer. Will set faster at 90°.	4–6 hours	5–7 hours
Resorcinol	Mix 3 parts powder to 4 parts liquid catalyst.	Apply thin coat to both surfaces and clamp.	Must be 70° or warmer. Sets faster at 90°.	8 hours	10 hours
Flake or powdered animal	For each ounce of glue, add 1½ ounces of water for softwood, 2 ounces for hardwood. Keep hot and use at 140°.	Apply with a brush and work fast. It is best to warm the joint for best results.	Must be 70° or warmer. A heat lamp is useful during assembly and setting period.	12 hours	24 hours

39

technique against the pointers shown here. Clamping deserves special attention—pressure should be evenly distributed and sufficient to squeeze out the excess glue but not so great as to starve the joint of adhesive by squeezing it dry.

Special Adhesives

Adhesives are used for more than the mere joining of wood to wood or metal to wood. There is a whole family of related adhesives designed for special purposes. Here are just a few of the "family;" they will be discussed more fully under their appropriate heading.

- wallpaper paste—comes ready mixed or in powder form and mixed with water; it is used to hold wallpaper to walls.
- linoleum paste and cement—generally the paste is used to hold linoleum roll goods or lino-

SELECTING THE BEST ADHESIVE FOR THE JOB

WORK TO BE GLUED	GLUE TO USE
Interior woodwork, furniture, cabinetwork	*Casein* *Hot hide glue* *Liquid hide glue* *Liquid fish glue* *Urea resin* *White polyvinyl liquid*
Exterior woodwork, patio or garden furniture and any work exposed to dampness	*Casein* *Resorcinol resin glue* *Urea resin*
General household gluing	*Cellulose household cement* *Casein, flexible latex* *Liquid fish glue* *Liquid hide glue* *Synthetic rubber and resin—all purpose type* *White polyvinyl liquid*
Laminating plastics to wood or plywood	*Synthetic rubber and resin—pressure sensitive type* *Resorcinol resin glue*
Metal cabinets to tile walls, metal to wood	*Synthetic rubber and resin—all purpose type and pressure sensitive type*
Oily woods, such as teak, rosewood, yew, lemonwood	*Casein* *Resorcinol resin glue*
Furniture repairs and patching	*Casein* *Hot hide glue* *Liquid fish glue* *Liquid hide glue* *Synthetic rubber and resin* *Urea resin* *White polyvinyl liquid*

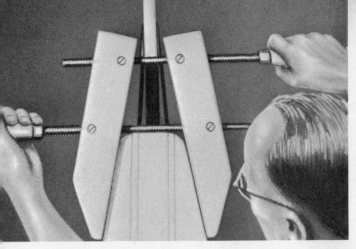

Uneven surfaces like this ironing-board end are clamped with ease with an adjustable hand screw. Screws are quickly opened or closed down to size by gripping both handles and cranking the screw in either direction.

leum tiles to floors; where moisture may be encountered, linoleum cement should be used.

- asphalt tile cement—these ready-mixed adhesives should be applied with a notched trowel; a gallon usually is sufficient to cover about 144 square feet.
- rubber tile cement—care should be taken to see that this adhesive is applied without lumps; a gallon should cover about 100 square feet.
- plastic tile mastic—mastic is just a special technical name for a type of glue or adhesive; you can cover about 50 square feet of floor with one gallon of mastic.
- metal tile cement—this special adhesive covers a more limited area than the other types of special adhesives; a gallon will be enough to cover about 32 square feet.

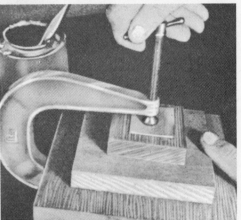

Deep-throated C clamps will reach into the center of small work where the pressure is most needed. These are all-metal construction and small wood pads must be used to protect the work from their jaws.

Photographs courtesy of Formica Company

Only light pressure is necessary when using a pressure-bonding adhesive. An ordinary household rolling pin will do the job, or use any hammer and a block of wood.

When applying a pressure-bonding synthetic rubber and resin adhesive (to bond a plastic laminate to plywood) use a notched spreader for an even distribution of the adhesive.

Air Conditioning

Air conditioning has added immeasurably to home comfort. Comfort, it seems, is achieved by an exacting combination of the right temperature with the right humidity, and neither one alone will do the trick. You can obtain this comfort in any room of your home in hot, humid weather by installing a room air conditioner. Or you can achieve greater comfort in every room by adding a home air conditioning unit.

Air conditioning does more than merely control the temperature and humidity. The better brand units also filter the air. Dust is removed, making it easier for the homemaker to keep her home clean. Irritating pollen is removed to bring relief to millions of hayfever sufferers. And today's air conditioners are exceedingly quiet. They help to cut out the outside noises and, at the same time, the motor operation of the unit itself is kept at a low noise level.

The Room Air Conditioner

Until recently, anyone adding a room air conditioner installed it at the base of the window. Depending upon the model, there was little choice—the unit would just bulge into the room and make the "window decorating" a problem. Other models projected out from the window and were an eye-sore from the exterior.

Today, you are no longer limited to the base of the window when you install air conditioning units. Furthermore, because of their more compact size and contemporary design, they blend into the room's furnishings and add to the decor instead of subtracting from it.

"Built-in" air conditioning is becoming exceedingly popular in many homes. The air conditioner is set into an exterior wall of the house and does not have to rob valuable window space. And the unit can be successfully disguised and "hidden" in the room. Even when it's not hidden, the modern styling enables it to blend in gracefully into any room's setting.

However, mounting the air conditioner in the window—whether it be at the base or along the top—is still the more common method of installing a room air conditioner. It is, by far, the simplest method of installation for the home handyman. How-

42

This Carrier air conditioner is unobtrusive in this room setting. Modern machines are small enough to be almost unnoticeable, while performing better than the big old units.

ever, if you are handy with tools and have the know-how, you can "build your air conditioner in the wall."

Home Air Conditioners

Whether you're building a new home or remodeling your existing home, you should investigate the possibility of adding a home air conditioning unit. In many cases, such a unit can be added to your existing heating system or as a supplement to it.

Here are some things to look for and questions to ask when you go to buy your central air conditioning unit.

1. *Variety of units*—There are three basic types of units—the year-round models which heat and cool the entire home from one cabinet and are designed primarily for new houses or replacement of worn-out furnaces; the conversion units for adapting forced warm air furnaces to year-round air conditioning; and the summer air conditioning units which are installed independently of the heating system.

2. *Survey and estimate*—A home air conditioning unit is not one for the average home handyman to install himself. He should secure the services of a reliable dealer. A good dealer will visit your home, draw a rough floor plan and estimate the cooling load needed for your home. He cannot tell you how much it will cost over the telephone.

3. *Humidity control*—An air conditioner's cooling coil lowers temperature and reduces humidity simultaneously. However, some systems will adequately control temperature but will not control humidity. Although the amount of surface of the

Traditional method of installing a room air conditioner is at the base of a window. Because the unit fits flush with the window, there's no decorating problem.

Casement windows no longer create a problem when mounting a room air conditioner. Note how easily this unit fits into the casement window, wihout cutting the metal frame.

cooling coil influences this, the basic factors in good humidity control are proper sizing of the unit and design of the system. When the air conditioner is too large for the amount of heat to be removed, it will turn itself off a good portion of the time and moisture will reevaporate from the cooling coil. When you're shopping for comfort, this is an important point to check with your dealer.

4. *Sturdy construction*—A central air conditioner should be ex-

43

HOW TO INSTALL A ROOM AIR CONDITIONER

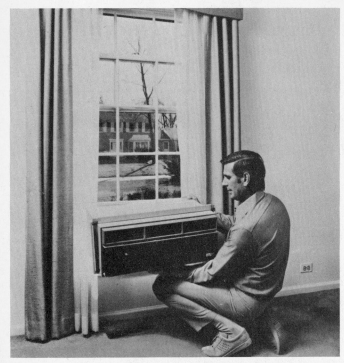

Unpack unit and place on window sill.

Pull out side "curtains" and screw in place.

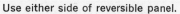

Use either side of reversible panel.

Set controls; all done. It's really easy.

pected to last a good long time and this requires sturdy construction of the cabinet as well as of other parts. While you can't be expected to tell the gage of the steel without a micrometer, a few taps on the cabinet can reassure you that it's of solid manufacture.

5. *Insulation*—The air conditioner's cabinet should be heavily insulated against sound and heat transmission. Look inside the unit. Certain portions of the ductwork which are exposed to non-air-conditioning space should also be insulated.

6. *Water use*—Some central air conditioners use water for refrigerant condensing and others have been developed which require no water at all. The reason is that some communities have legislated against water consumption for air conditioning. In other areas, water is simply in short supply, expensive, or difficult to dispose of, or may become so in some easily foreseeable future time. One air conditioned home on a block may not present much of a strain on the available water supply, but a dozen might. The best way to decide which type of unit you should obtain is to check with your local water supply company or city department as well as the dealer.

The "New Look" with Air Conditioned Homes

An extensive recent survey indicates that changes, both interior and exterior, are beginning to appear in homes designed around air conditioning.

The most obvious exterior design changes are related to turning back the heat of the sun. More roofs are being painted white and roof over-

Exterior view of modern window airconditioning unit shows how little space it takes, and how little of the view it really spoils—hence this unit's name, "Viewsaver."

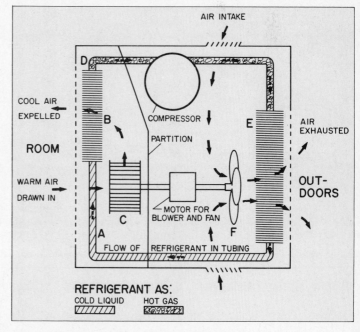

Diagram shows operation of air-conditioner.

In many homes, solid walls can be used on some exposures, providing valuable space for built-ins, and other exposures can be entirely of glass for view and light.

hangs are being extended to protect window's from the sun's glare. Orientation of windows is getting more attention from builders and architects.

Indoors, the changes are most apparent in terms of greater convenience. For example, take the bedroom which is usually difficult to furnish because it requires so much furniture in such a small space. In addition,

Decorating colors can be lighter if the room is air conditioned, since much of the normal grime and dirt are eliminated.

Windows need no longer break up an efficient kitchen cabinet arrangement. They can be placed over the sink where most housewives like them, leaving the other walls solid.

Since air conditioning makes cross-ventilation unnecessary, bedroom windows do not interfere with furniture placement.

walls are frequently broken up by standard double-hung windows necessary to provide good ventilation. With air conditioning, windows can be moved up on the wall to give greater privacy as well as more wall space for furniture.

Similar changes can be found in living areas. Imagine a living-room with a wall entirely of glass facing south—an exposure which can be satisfactorily shielded from the sun by roof overhang. Another wall without windows faces west where the afternoon heat of the sun through glass would be intense. This solid wall can now be used for built-ins or a convenient furniture arrangement.

The kitchen is the hottest room in the home and ordinarily needs a good deal of cross-ventilation. But scattering windows around the walls plays havoc with efficient arrangement of cabinets and working space. With air conditioning cross-ventilation is no longer necessary and the window area can be confined to one wall. An exhaust fan over the range takes away cooking odors.

Air conditioning can also recover what might once have been considered virtually unusable space, and permit its use on the same basis as other areas of the house. This is particularly true of the basement, where dampness, mildew, rust and dirt have frequently hampered its full use as a hobby, recreation, activity or even storage area. But an air conditioned basement properly protected against leakage of water from outside can become a completely enjoyable part of the home.

Selecting the Size of a Room Air Conditioner

The following simple method of determining the proper size air conditioner for a room is suggested by Carrier Corporation. It requires only four calculations to arrive at the total cooling units required. Simply fill in the figures requested below, multiply by the special multiplier and place the answer in the right hand column. When finished, add up the right hand

1. Windows
Count the number of windows on which the sun shines at any time during the day and enter the total here.

_____ × 500 = _____

Count the number of windows which face north or are in the shade all day and enter the total here.

_____ × 250 = _____

2. Floor Area
Compute the number of square feet of floor area of the space to be cooled and enter the total here.

_____ × 30 = _____

3. Uninsulated Roof
If the space to be cooled is under an uninsulated roof exposed to the sun, enter the same square footage as above.

_____ × 9 = _____

To select the proper size unit, add all the totals and consult the following table.

Up to 4,700 Cooling Units requires a 1/3 HP unit.
4,800 to 7,100 Cooling Units requires a 1/2 HP unit.
7,200 to 11,100 Cooling Units requires a 3/4 HP unit.
11,200 to 14,200 Cooling Units requires a 1 HP unit.
14,300 to 20,000 Cooling Units requires a 1 1/2 HP unit.

49

This conversion unit, designed for a down-flow forced warm air furnace, is shown installed in a first floor closet of a house with no basement. The furnace is lifted a few inches to allow the small counterflow coil to go underneath.

The conversion unit pictured below adapts a warm air heating system to year-round air conditioning. It is placed in the basement and used with a standard vertical furnace.

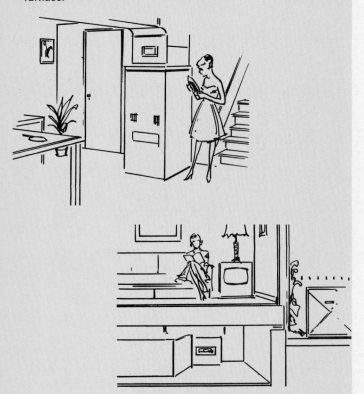

Here the conversion unit is added to a horizontal forced warm air furnace, installed in the crawl space of a house with no basement.

column and the job is done. Residential windows are based on an average of 12 square feet each.

Adding Central Air Conditioning to the Home

Economical air conditioning of any kind of house is now possible with the introduction of new central air conditioning equipment. The last large category of existing homes previously considered difficult or expensive to air condition—those with hot water or steam heat and those without central heating systems—can now add summer cooling at a reasonable cost without modifying the heating equipment.

Practically all homes fall into one of the following five categories as far as heating systems are concerned.

1. If you live in a home with warm water or steam heat using radiators or one of the other radiant heat applications, you can install a summer air conditioner such as the Summer Weathermaker. The small unit located inside the house contains cooling and dehumidifying coils, filter and air-circulation fan. It can be hung from the ceiling in a hallway, closet or utility room, or placed in a minimum space in the attic, basement or crawl space.

The simplest kind of duct system can be used because perimeter discharge of air which is usually advisable for heating systems in cool climates is not necessary for cooling. It is connected to a refrigerating unit requiring no water which is located outside.

2. If your house has a floor furnace or space heaters, the approach is the same as for houses with wet heat.

3. If you have a modern forced

warm air heating system in good condition, you can obtain year-round air conditioning at a comparatively low cost. You can install a conversion unit which uses the furnace and existing duct system for filtering and air circulation and adds cooling and dehumidifying. There are models available which can be installed with any kind of forced warm air furnace, whether, it is the standard vertical type, counterflow or down-flow unit, or a horizontal heating plant installed in a crawl space or attic.

The small, quiet cooling and dehumidifying coil package is located at the discharge end of the furnace, and a weatherproof and tamperproof refrigerating unit requiring no water is placed out of doors.

4. If you have a forced warm air furnace which is getting old and worn, it might be better to replace it with a summer and winter unit like the Year-Round Weathermaker than to try to convert it. You can usually use the same duct system. This is less expensive than installing a new forced warm air unit and adding a conversion unit later on.

The complete unit handles both summer and winter air conditioning. It supplies cooling, dehumidifying, heating, air circulation and filtering. A simple control shifts it from cooling to heating and the same thermostat sets the temperature level for summer and winter. It is available either with air-cooled refrigeration using no water, or water-cooled, and for heating it burns oil or gas.

5. If you have an old gravity warm air furnace with warm air pipes coming off in all directions, your best bet is to replace it completely with a unit which will provide winter and summer air conditioning. Conversion is not recommended. Some modification will be necessary in the ducts and outlets, but you would need this if you installed a new forced warm air system.

Aluminum

Do-It-Yourself Aluminum comes in a great variety of shapes and sizes including plain and embossed sheets, tubing, rod, angle, bar and clear plastic sheet. Aluminum hardware consists of corner locks, screen and storm sash hanging devices, machine screws, wood screws, sheet metal screws and rivets.

Special extruded shapes are available for storm sash and screen frame members featuring aluminum splines for screen or sheet plastic storm sash construction. Rain gutters and downspouts as well as the hardware to mount them are stock items.

Many finishes and textures can be given to the aluminum surface by grinding, polishing, scratch brushing, buffing, burnishing, tumbling, highlighting, fluting, sandblasting, embossing and spin finishing. Paints, enamels, varnishes and lacquers can also be used after the surface is cleaned for proper bonding.

Marking Tools

Marking tools are probably the first tools which you will use to plan your layouts and designs. A scratch awl, a pair of dividers, a steel rule, a pencil, crayon or sharp nail may be used for marking the aluminum. Avoid scribing too deeply.

A flat steel square will work better

51

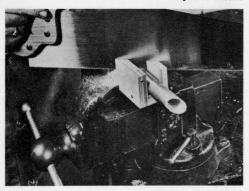

*Photograph courtesy of
Reynolds Metals*

Regular wood handsaws work well in cutting Do-It-Yourself Aluminum. Fine-toothed saws are recommended. Lubricate saw with paraffin for smooth cuts.

Ordinary kitchen shears shown above can cut through sheet aluminum.

52

than the combination wood and metal square because it will be in full contact with the working surface and will contribute to greater accuracy. Always tip on edge any thick measuring devices such as yardsticks or zigzag rules to get accurate pin point measurements.

Cutting Tools

Cutting tools for your aluminum projects will depend upon the thickness and shape of the stock you are using.

For tubes, rods, bars and extruded shapes, a good wood saw or hacksaw will do. The more teeth per inch on the saw blade the finer and neater the cut.

Irregular curved lines can be cut with precision and fine edges with a coping, scroll or jeweler's saw.

A pocket knife will remove burrs from inside tubes and can be used for small interior cuts on the plain and embossed sheets.

An ordinary pair of household scissors or combination tin snips will cut the plain and embossed sheet aluminum easily and accurately.

Small interior areas can be cut cleanly and neatly with a sharp cold chisel or a wood chisel. The metal should be laid over a piece of smooth scrap wood to save the tool edge when using a wood chisel. Long-toothed single-cut files which do not clog up are effective cutting tools. A file card or steel brush will keep the teeth clean.

Auger bits in a carpenter's brace or a hand drill with twist drills will cut screw, rivet and larger holes. All sheets must be backed with scrap wood for neat, clean holes. Drilling accuracy in sheet, bar, tube or angle stock will be guaranteed if you use a center punch or nail tapped lightly to give the bit a resting place.

Your regular wood planes are suitable for dressing down the aluminum stock of sheet, bar or angle material. Always make a light cut and repeat cuts to get greater depth of cut.

A wood expansion bit backed up with smooth scrap wood will cut the large holes efficiently and cleanly in sheet stock.

Forming Tools and Jigs

Various hammers and mallets are useful in bending and forming aluminum sheet metal, bars, and angle stock. Plastic tipped, rubber, wood and rawhide mallets will prevent marring and marking your projects. A light ball peen hammer will do double duty in clinching rivets, forming shallow trays and coasters and in planishing. Planishing is the name given to the process of making a hammered and dimpled effect on metal with a ball peen hammer or other shaped hammer.

Pliers and wrenches used for holding and twisting the metal should have their jaws padded with tape to prevent marring. Wooden and metal jigs for bending, forming and holding the metal stock are described in more

A wood expansion bit bores clean holes through the Do-It-Yourself sheet aluminum. Back-up the sheet metal with a smooth wood block as shown above.

detail in the section on Forming and Fastening Aluminum.

Your regular selection of screwdrivers and wrenches will take care of the screws, nuts and bolts which will be used on your projects.

Power Tools

BENCH SAW—A bench saw with any of the following accessories will take care of all cuts necessary in your projects; regular wood or metal blades, i.e., combination, rip or crosscut, emery wheel used on saw and sanding discs.

When feeding your aluminum stock into the blade on a bench saw the work may tend to rise up from

A wood working block plane may be used for smoothing or trimming edges. Use a light cut for best results.

53

the saw. This can be overcome by making a wood plate from a small section of plywood and clamping or screwing it to the saw fence.

The blade should be permitted to cut into the wood plate. This jig will not only eliminate the metal's tendency to climb, but it will also protect you from flying metal chips.

BAND SAW AND JIG SAW— The band saw used with the standard wood blades or metal cutting blades plus a back-up board for stack cutting will give neat, accurate results. A thin sheet of wood under the aluminum stock when jig-sawing will prevent chatter, binding and ragged edges. Your jig-saw can be used with the regular blades, with metal cutting blades or the jig-saw file set.

DRILL PRESS—The drill press can be used with twist drills, wood bits or circular cutters as well as to buff and polish your finished projects. To use auger bits in the drill press grind the lead screw to a point. Power wood bits will cut aluminum more effectively if a pilot hole is drilled first to receive the tip of the bit.

Carefully center punch all holes before drilling and be sure to clamp your work to the press table with a smooth piece of scrap wood underneath.

The sunswirl effect seen on compacts, cigarette cases is also a decorative device you can make on your aluminum projects with the drill press or hand power tool.

To make the sunswirl tool, cement a soft disc of rubber to the end of a ½″ dowel and glue a circular piece of emery cloth to the rubber pad. Chuck the dowel in the press and run it slowly while raising and lowering the press handle.

Buffing and polishing on aluminum projects can be done on the drill press as well as with a portable power drill.

JOINTER—Used with the standard blades your jointer will dress down the longer pieces of angle and bar aluminum stock. As with the hand plane, set the blades for a shallow cut and use oil or paraffin on the metal surfaces to reduce drag.

Forming Do-It-Yourself Aluminum

Any mallet that's smooth and soft such as plastic, rubber, wood or rawhide will provide a good neat working surface. To bend sheet metal lay it over the edge of a smooth board and gently mallet it to the angle desired.

A sheet bending jig for special projects may be made by sawing a slot or groove lengthwise into a piece of wood with a bench saw. The slot or groove is cut to the depth of the required bend or brake.

A simple jig can be fashioned from two boards clamped to either side of the metal at the proper depth while another board or mallet is used to

54

A coping, scroll or jeweler's saw will cut mitre corners as well as curves, scrolls and designs in the aluminum stock.

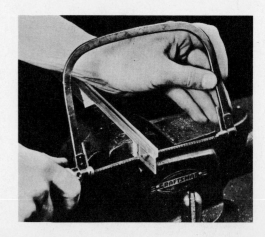

turn the metal over. A section of angle iron or aluminum clamped to the smooth sharp edge of a board or work bench will hold the sheet firmly for malleting.

To roll edges, saw a slot lengthwise in a dowel, broom handle, pipe or any cylindrical object of desired size. Insert the sheet in the slot and wrap around by hand.

Shallow ash trays and coasters can be formed from discs of sheet metal by using the end grain of a block of wood clamped in a vise as a back-up and tapping the metal gently with a hammer in a circular motion. The disc must be kept at a constant angle until the metal has been tapped in a complete circle. Hammering cold metal will make it hard and brittle, so practice on some scraps before you tackle your job.

Bending solid rods, bars, and tubes can be accomplished in a vise with various hand tools and with simple jigs which you can make from scrap wood in a few minutes. To use your metal-working vise on aluminum projects, cover the jaws of the vise with scraps of aluminum to prevent marring and chewing of the material you are working.

To make 45° or 90° angles with bar or rod stock, clamp the metal parallel to the vise jaws and push the extended end of the material with one hand while striking the metal near the vise with a mallet. A block of wood with a hole drilled through it slightly larger than the rod stock makes a good bending jig.

Bar stock can also be bent in a wood block which has had a notch

---

The smallest radius to which it is possible to bend the various diameter tubes filled with sand are:

DIAMETER OF TUBE	SMALLEST RADIUS
¾"	2½"
1"	4¾"
1¾"	5½"

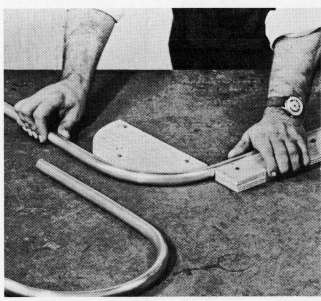

Simple jigs made from plywood or scrap blocks and boards are used to bend your aluminum stock in a variety of shapes and sizes.

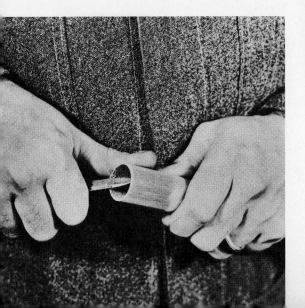

An ordinary pocket knife as shown above will cut and trim aluminum. Burrs are easily removed from tubes, bars, rods and angle metal.

Simple cutting, bending, and finishing operations produce these decorative items from sheet aluminum.

cut into it and secured in a vise. Use a mallet to get sharp bends.

A round wooden jig cut from scrap plywood with a notch in it, anchored to the bench, will form circles and curves.

Twists for furniture legs and decorative effects are made by fastening one end of an aluminum bar in the vise, covering the bar with a length of pipe and then twisting with a wrench or pliers at the free end of the bar. The length of pipe over the bar stock will hold the aluminum straight while the twists are forming.

An exact square corner on the inside of a bar bend is formed by sawing a small slot in the exact position where the bar is to be bent.

Jigs for forming tubes, rods and bars in curves are cut from scrap boards or plywood. Draw your pattern on the wood and remove the excess wood with a jig-saw or coping saw. On a level, rigid surface, fasten the pattern with nails, screws or bolts. At a distance equal to the thickness of the stock being formed and at the beginning of the curve

fasten a small block of wood as an anchor point in your jig. Be sure the anchor block is located at the beginning of the curve. Insert your stock between the anchor block and the curved jig and slowly bend.

Sharp curves in aluminum tubes can be made without buckling the walls if you fill the tubes with damp sand before bending. To do this, insert a wooden stopper in one end of the aluminum tubing, then take a bucket of wet sand and push the tube into the bucket, tamping with the tube until it is firmly packed with sand. Form the curves and bends very slowly in your jig. This operation must be done slowly and carefully because, in bending a tube, the metal on the outside wall of the tube is being stretched while the metal on the inner wall of the tube is being compressed. Bending too fast will result in buckling on the inner wall, rupturing on the outer wall, flattening or all three.

A free-hand method of bending tubes and rods is to place smooth dowels in a block of wood, two steel pins in a block of steel or two bolts in a vise, slightly farther apart

Wall Primitives can be cut from embossed aluminum.

than the thickness of the stock, and pull slowly and steadily on the free end of the stock.

Angle stock for special projects can be formed from strips of sheet metal in a vise or bending jig. Angle aluminum can be bent by drilling a hole at the point where the bend is to be made and cutting away a wedge of metal to the angle desired. The bend is then formed around a length of rod or dowel of the proper size.

Mitred corners in angle stock can be formed by cutting away a wedge of metal on one leg of the angle stock and bending in a vise with the help of a mallet.

Fastening Do-It-Yourself Aluminum

There are a number of ways to join the different shapes and sizes of aluminum stock using rivets, clips, tabs and slots, grooved seams, screws and nuts and bolts.

RIVETS—First choose the proper size drill to make the hole for the rivets. The shank of the drill should match the body of the rivet for a good tight fit. The proper length for

the rivet to hold properly and firmly should be approximately one and one half times the thickness of the rivet.

Insert the rivet into the drilled holes and make sure that the sheets being joined are drawn together. Back-up the rivet with a piece of

Try making one of these fascinating "mobiles" for a Christmas decoration.

There is no limit to the variety of party decorations that you can make.

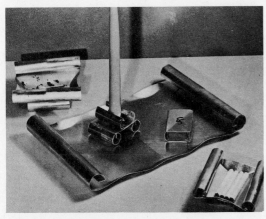

An attractive desk set can be made easily and quickly.

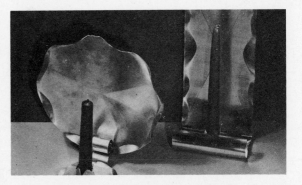

The attractive surface patterns on these two candlestick holders and reflectors are produced by masking off sections separately and sandpapering them lightly or rubbing with steel wool.

steel and with the ball end of your ball peen hammer, mushroom the end of the rivet. Follow this procedure until you have completed joining the sheets. Smooth all rivet ends with a power tool, fine sandpaper or emery cloth.

GROOVED SEAM—The simplest method of joining two pieces of sheet metal is the grooved seam. To do this, first fold over the corresponding edges an equal amount, hook the lips together then with a mallet and block of wood, hammer them together. A few dimples along the seam made with a hammer and center punch or nail will prevent the seam from working loose.

In working on some of your projects, you may find it necessary to join a bar to a rod with a rivet. Your joint will be simple and strong if you form a shoulder on the rod by sawing or filing a flat surface on the rod then joining the two pieces and drilling a hole for the rivet.

The procedure just mentioned is followed to make a swivel joint on two rods, except that both rods are filed flat and then drilled and riveted.

Angles can be joined to metal sheets with self-tapping screws, sheet metal screws or in some cases nuts and bolts.

There are a number of methods of joining sheet metal to tubes. One is to slit the tube lengthwise, insert the sheet metal into the slot and secure with a sheet metal or self-tapping screw. The sheet metal can also be kept firmly in position by inserting dowel rods into either end of the tubing.

Tubing can be used for a leg or stand by making four flaps in the end of the tube, bending them over and placing screws through the flaps into the piece of wood or metal to be supported.

Corner gussets can be used to join angles or bars with rivets or nuts and bolts. When you bend a piece of angle aluminum to make a corner, the wedge of metal cut from the angle leg can be used as the reinforcing gusset for that corner.

When it is necessary to join two ends of a bar as in trimming counter tops a dovetail joint will hold firmly and neatly. Mark the joint carefully and accurately with a scratch awl, then cut with a saw on the inside of your markings, then carefully file away excess metal for a perfect, tight joint.

A hinge may easily be cut and bent, using a piece of wire coat hanger for the hinge pin. Many intricate designs and antique hinges can be easily made of aluminum for any of your projects. When measuring the tab allowance, mark off 3½

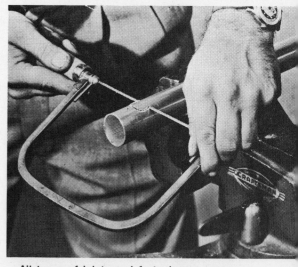

All types of joints and fastenings are possible with this type of aluminum. Shown above a coping saw is used to cut an opening in aluminum tubing for a right angle joint made with two different diameter tubes.

58

times the diameter of the wire on each side. Always make an odd number of sections to equalize the strain.

In many cases, for decorative effects, you may wish to join two sections of sheet metal together with a clip. To make this joint, bend back both edges an equal amount, from another piece of metal form a clip by determining the amount of bend necessary to draw the two sheets firmly together. Force the clip onto the bent sheet edges with a mallet, level and tighten the clip by malleting over with a smooth block of wood and dimple with a nail or center punch for added strength.

A favorite woodworker's joint, the cross-lap, can also be utilized with Do-It-Yourself aluminum bars and rods. Here again as with the dovetail joint extreme care is necessary for an accurate joint. Mark the pieces with a scratch awl, saw inside the awl marks and finish with a file, checking frequently for a proper fit. Aluminum tubes can be joined to many flat surfaces such as wood, angle metal, sheet metal, bars and other material by squeezing the end of the tube flat in a vise and drilling for screw holes. Tubes can be joined to wood for legs by using the above method or by inserting a section of wood dowel in the end of the tube and running a screw through the tube, dowel and into the wood. Tubes can be lengthened by inserting a plug part way into one end of the tube and forcing another section of tubing over the wood plug. Screws can be driven into the tube section to give added strength.

A "T" joint or other butt joint can be made with aluminum tubing if the tube end is fitted with a dowel. This tube end is then marked and cut with a scroll saw and a half-round file to the outside dimensions of the tube it will be joined to. A long wood screw is then driven through the tubes for a long-lasting tight joint. A variety of joints and fastenings can be devised for the Do-It-Yourself Aluminum. You will find that as you begin to work with this metal you will develop special joints and fastenings to suit the particular projects you are working on. There are also special elbows, T-butt and flanges available, made of aluminum, to fit all sizes of tubes.

Helpful Hints

On all of your aluminum projects, use only aluminum nails, screws and other hardware made of aluminum. If these materials aren't available, then use chrome- or cadmium-plated hardware to avoid an unsightly rust or corrosion.

Before you tackle any original designs or ideas, draw and lay out the project on heavy paper or light cardboard. The paper or cardboard can be bent or folded to follow your design. In this way you will avoid wasting any metal and can make corrections before a single piece of metal is measured and cut. In addition, the corrected test pattern can then be used to lay out your project on the metal to scale.

When you file sheet edges or other thin pieces of metal, move your file as nearly parallel to the edge of the metal as possible. This method will give you long clean cuts, your file won't chatter and bind and your strokes will give you a continuous even surface.

59

A typical do-it-yourself project is the making of aluminum and glass or plastic shower doors. The drawings show step-by-step building and installation of such doors. The techniques used for working with the aluminum in this project can be applied to a wide variety of other projects as well. Plans are given on the following pages.

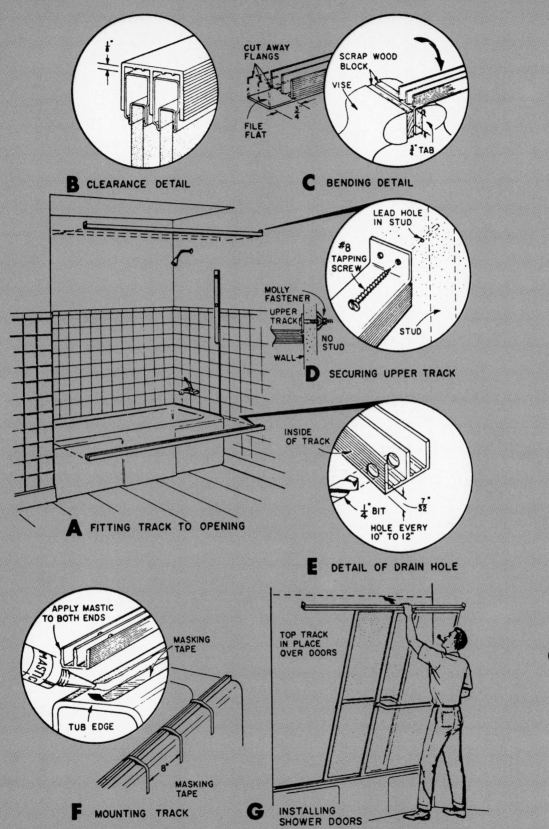

B CLEARANCE DETAIL

C BENDING DETAIL

CUT AWAY FLANGS

FILE FLAT

SCRAP WOOD BLOCK

VISE

¾" TAB

A FITTING TRACK TO OPENING

MOLLY FASTENER

UPPER TRACK

WALL

NO STUD

LEAD HOLE IN STUD

#8 TAPPING SCREW

STUD

D SECURING UPPER TRACK

INSIDE OF TRACK

¼" BIT

$\frac{7}{32}$"

HOLE EVERY 10" TO 12"

E DETAIL OF DRAIN HOLE

APPLY MASTIC TO BOTH ENDS

MASTIC

MASKING TAPE

TUB EDGE

8"

MASKING TAPE

F MOUNTING TRACK

TOP TRACK IN PLACE OVER DOORS

G INSTALLING SHOWER DOORS

61

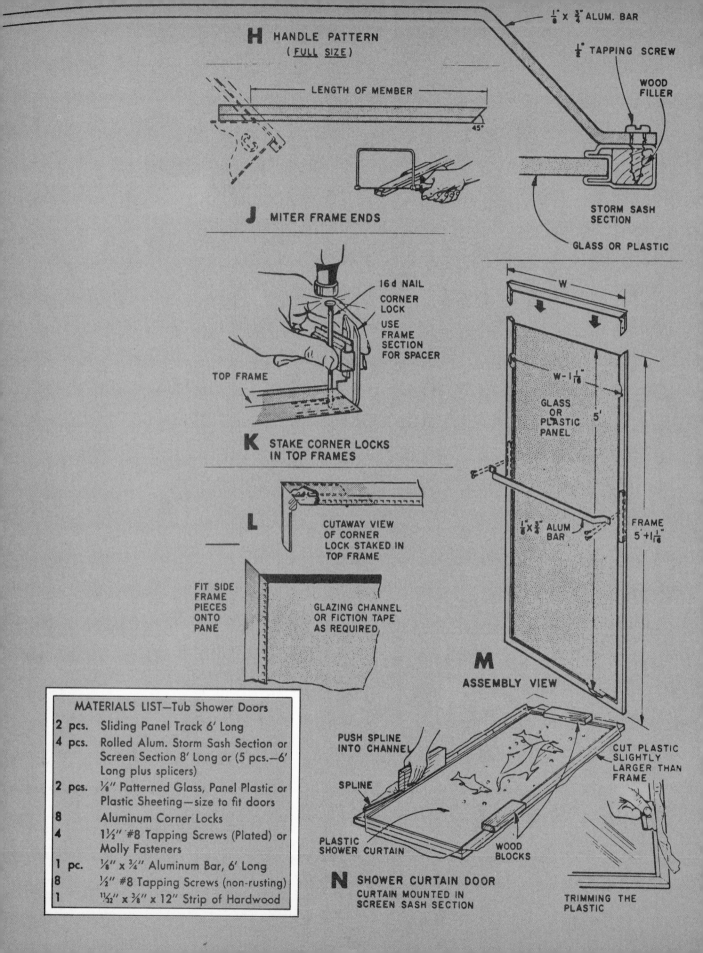

H HANDLE PATTERN
(FULL SIZE)

⅛" x ¾" ALUM. BAR

½" TAPPING SCREW

WOOD FILLER

LENGTH OF MEMBER

45°

J MITER FRAME ENDS

STORM SASH SECTION

GLASS OR PLASTIC

16 d NAIL

CORNER LOCK

USE FRAME SECTION FOR SPACER

TOP FRAME

K STAKE CORNER LOCKS IN TOP FRAMES

W

W−1 1⁄16"

GLASS OR PLASTIC PANEL

5'

⅛" x ¾" ALUM. BAR

FRAME 5' +1 1⁄16"

L

CUTAWAY VIEW OF CORNER LOCK STAKED IN TOP FRAME

FIT SIDE FRAME PIECES ONTO PANE

GLAZING CHANNEL OR FICTION TAPE AS REQUIRED

M ASSEMBLY VIEW

MATERIALS LIST—Tub Shower Doors

2 pcs.	Sliding Panel Track 6' Long
4 pcs.	Rolled Alum. Storm Sash Section or Screen Section 8' Long or (5 pcs.—6' Long plus splicers)
2 pcs.	⅛" Patterned Glass, Panel Plastic or Plastic Sheeting—size to fit doors
8	Aluminum Corner Locks
4	1½" #8 Tapping Screws (Plated) or Molly Fasteners
1 pc.	⅛" x ¾" Aluminum Bar, 6' Long
8	½" #8 Tapping Screws (non-rusting)
1	11⁄32" x ⅜" x 12" Strip of Hardwood

PUSH SPLINE INTO CHANNEL

SPLINE

PLASTIC SHOWER CURTAIN

WOOD BLOCKS

CUT PLASTIC SLIGHTLY LARGER THAN FRAME

N SHOWER CURTAIN DOOR
CURTAIN MOUNTED IN SCREEN SASH SECTION

TRIMMING THE PLASTIC

Anatomy for Building

As a basic guide for the handymen interested in making their own kitchen cabinets, designing and building their own furniture or constructing built-ins for their home, here are the important standard measurements. While it is possible to rely upon your eye for judging graceful lines or proper proportions, there are certain dimensions in building for the home that are universal. They are followed by all architects, industrial designers and furniture designers. The seat of a chair, for example, must be 15″ to 18″ above the floor and the back must slope at an angle of 105° to the seat, if the chair is to be comfortable to sit in. That is comfortable for adults; for an average child of 11, the seat should be 14″ above the floor level.

Naturally, you take the dimensions of the chairs in your home for granted just as you do the height of the kitchen cabinets above the sink or the range. Yet, certain basic dimensions have been used by the people who planned them. In today's home, with the handyman doing more and more building, it is necessary for him to have these basic figures readily available.

The accompanying illustrations are an introduction to the art of planning, the anatomy of building. There are several comprehensive volumes readily available in libraries or in bookshops, which can supply the more advanced handyman with additional dimensions.

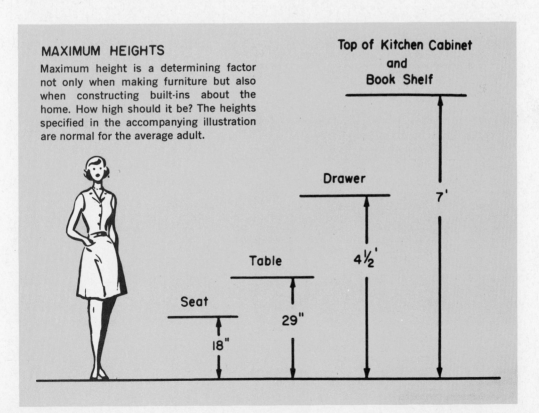

MAXIMUM HEIGHTS

Maximum height is a determining factor not only when making furniture but also when constructing built-ins about the home. How high should it be? The heights specified in the accompanying illustration are normal for the average adult.

Top of Kitchen Cabinet and Book Shelf

Drawer

7'

4½'

Table

Seat

29"

18"

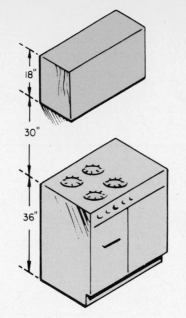

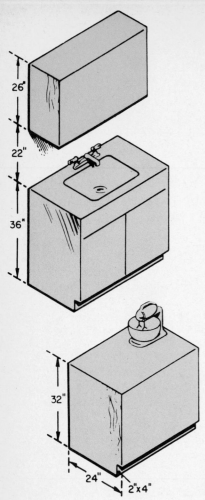

FOR FOOD PREPARATION

Efficient kitchen operation depends to a great extent upon the height of base cabinets. Toe space, along the lower front, is needed so that the housekeeper can work close to the cabinets. The most efficient height of counters used for food preparation is 32" above the floor. Near the sink and range, however, base cabinets should be about 36" from floor level, so that the tops of the cabinets are aligned with the appliances.

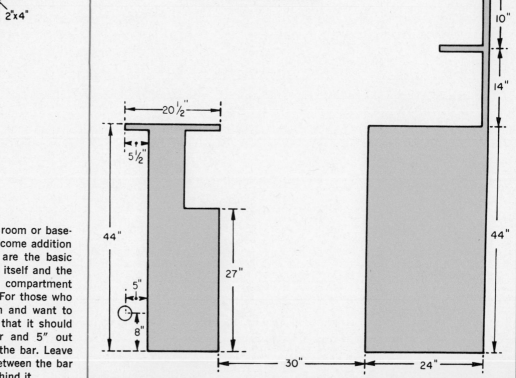

FOR PLAYROOM BARS

A bar in the recreation room or basement play area is a welcome addition to many homes. Here are the basic dimensions for the bar itself and the accompanying storage compartment and shelves behind it. For those who like a touch of realism and want to add a brass rail, note that it should be 8" above the floor and 5" out from the front face of the bar. Leave adequate aisle space between the bar and the storage wall behind it.

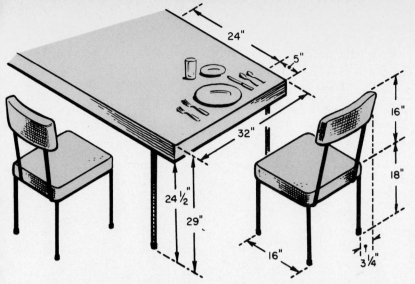

	Table Height	Chair Height
	— in inches —	
Adults	29	18
14 to 18 years	26	16
8 to 14 years	24	14
4 to 8 years	22	12

Elbow room is an important factor when planning a family dining table. There must be sufficient space not only for the place setting but for serving trays and dishes as well. Extra space never goes to waste.

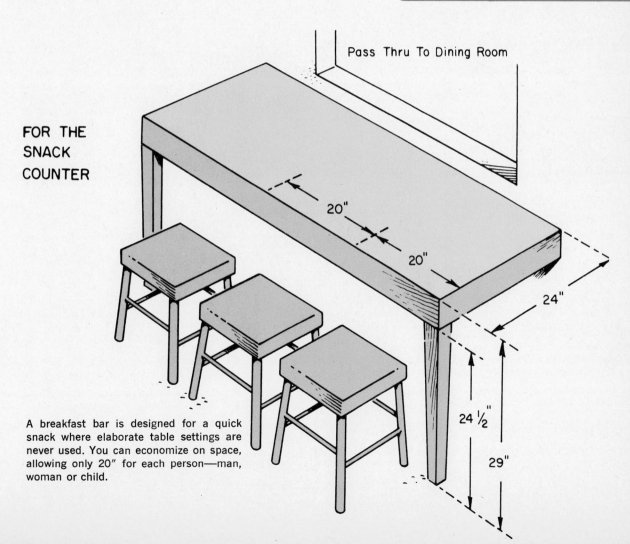

FOR THE SNACK COUNTER

Pass Thru To Dining Room

A breakfast bar is designed for a quick snack where elaborate table settings are never used. You can economize on space, allowing only 20″ for each person—man, woman or child.

Anatomy for the Workshop

The right height for your workbench and your power tools is, to a great extent, determined by your height and your working habits. It is essential that the workbench be at a convenient height, one that will minimize fatigue, make the work easy to get at and be at the right level for various hand tool operations.

When mounting power tools on a stand, the correct height is important not only from a craftsman's viewpoint but also for safety's sake. In table form are some average heights for a workbench plus power tool stands. Remember, these are only averages; adjust them to meet your own needs.

Heights for the Workshop

Workbench	36″-40″
Table Saw	36″-38″
Shaper	36″
Jointer	32″-34″
Drill Press	48″
Band Saw	38″-40″
Jig Saw	38″-40″
Belt-Disc Sander	32″-34″
Lathe	38″-40″
Grinder	34″-36″

Anchors for Walls
For Masonry

There are several ways for the handyman to attach wood or metal to masonry, either concrete or brick. He encounters this type of an anchoring problem when he:

- installs studding or furring strips prior to erecting walls for a finished basement.
- adds metal shelf brackets inside a concrete block garage.
- secures electrical conduit to the outside of a brick house. The

There are many varieties of anchors for use in concrete and masonry. Above are some of the more commonly used ones. At right is a stud driver, the Ammo Drive Tool.

66

most commonly used method of anchoring to concrete or brick is the lag bolt and anchor unit. The anchor, which resembles a tube, can be made of lead, fiber or plastic. It is necessary to drill a hole in the masonry with a star drill and hammer or a masonry bit and electric drill before inserting the anchor.

But if you wish to avoid the drilling of holes for anchors, you can use:

- *steel cut nails.* Hammer the nail through the piece of wood to be joined to a brick joint or concrete block surface.
- *concrete nails,* which have heavy fluted shanks. When using these, pre-drill the wood to avoid splitting.
- *adhesive nails,* which resemble oversized thumb tacks with perforated square heads. A blob of adhesive spread over the head secures it to the concrete or brick. The board is then driven onto the protruding nail, which is clinched to secure the board.

Still another type of fastening device employs a tool into which a stud or pin is inserted, then driven into a wall with a hammer. Simple to use and requiring no special skill, this type of tool has proven popular with do-it-yourselfers for fastening to concrete, concrete block or brick walls. On brick walls, the studs or pins must be driven into the mortar joints. For the average handyman's purposes, these driving tools are a good investment, particularly where a large project like a basement finishing is involved. They will pay for themselves many times over in aggravation spared.

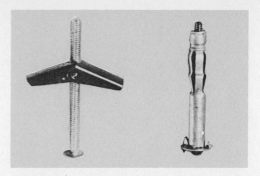

Spring and solid head toggle bolts are used for anchoring to walls where the surface is too thin to retain a screw or nail.

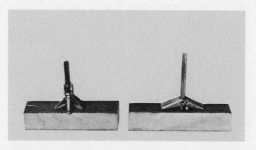

What they look like from the other side— on left is a Molly fastener. Note how spider legs draw up toward the head to hold this anchor in place. Spring toggle (right) is also an efficient wall anchor. Note hole through piece of wood (or wall when you are using it) must be large enough for the spring head to pass through in a folded position.

For Hollow Walls

While a picture hook, nail or screw is usually sufficient to secure a picture or mirror to a wall, there are times when the weight of the object to be hung is too great to use these anchoring devices safely. Unless the nail or screw goes through the wall into wood (either a stud or lath), it will be unable to do the job.

The technique of securing a wall anchor depends, in part, upon the type of material used for the wall. For a plaster wall, you can drill a hole, insert a Rawl plug and then set

67

a screw into it. This is similar to the lag bolt and anchor method used in masonry.

However, with the greater use of dry wall construction in homes to-day—plasterboard, Sheetrock, plywood—another more positive form of wall anchor is needed. These are Mollies, a special anchoring device which expands inside the wall. Mollies are made for use in plaster or dry walls. Here, in step by step form, is the technique for attaching any anchor of this type:

- Drill a hole in the wall of the same diameter as the Molly.
- Remove the screw from the anchor and hammer the body of the anchor into the wall. Make certain that the teeth under the anchor head are imbedded in the wall material.
- Replace the screw and tighten as far as possible. This action compresses the anchor within the wall.
- After the anchor is secured, remove the screw and set it through the bracket or wood to be attached to the wall; then place the end of the screw into the hole in the anchor. Tighten the screw until the work is secured to the wall.

Toggle bolts can also be used when a material or object must be secured to plaster, gypsum wallboard or other surface of thin material that will not directly retain a screw or nail. There are two types of toggle bolts, spring head and solid head. The holding power varies with the type of bolt and increases with size. The screw section of the bolt cannot be removed without loss of the anchor, as can be done with the Molly fastener.

Antiquing

Antiquing is one of the easiest ways to refinish furniture. This glazing technique was once used primarily to add a mellow, aged look to newer pieces of furniture. It is now even more popular when used to create other startling effects. The cast-off furniture pieces on these pages are dramatic examples.

There are three steps to antiquing or glazing: (1) The surface is painted a background color and allowed to dry hard. (2) A colored glazing liquid is brushed over one section at a time, then partially wiped off with cheesecloth or other material to give a streaked or smeared effect. (3) A coat of low-luster clear varnish is applied to protect the finish.

The materials used are inexpensive, and by buying them separately, they offer a wider choice of colors than with a kit. You can duplicate the handsome results by following these directions.

Basic Materials

1 pint satin-finish enamel
½ pint glazing liquid
1 tube tinting oil color
Paint thinner
Paint brushes
Container for mixing glaze
Cheesecloth or other wiping material
Sandpaper and/or steel wool
Mixing paddles

The How-To

Before beginning to paint, prepare the old surface by cleaning off all wax, grease and dirt with paint thinner and a rag. You usually don't have to remove the old finish. Patch or fill wherever required and, if the

finish is glossy, rough up the surface with sandpaper and/or steel wool. Unless the surface is peeling or chipping, this is all that is necessary. A quick test to make sure the surface is in good condition is to draw a coin against the grain. If the finish flakes off, use sanding liquid or surface preparer as directed on container.

1. For the base coat, brush on a satin-finish enamel. If the new color differs greatly from the old, a second coat may be necessary. Bleeding may occur with some mahogany pieces. It is then necessary to apply a pigmented stain killer first, before the coat. In selecting the base color remember that, after the glaze is applied over it, the intensity of the base color will be diminished and its cast, or tone, may be changed. Choose a brighter color than you'll want in the end and try to visualize the effect the glaze will have (a white glaze over a red background will give a pink effect and so on).

It is important to allow the base coat to dry until completely hard before glazing. Follow the directions on the label, but ideally you should allow the base coat to dry for 24 hours. At the same time, apply the base coat to back or other inconspicuous surfaces, or even scrap wood. This will be a test surface for experimenting with the glaze.

2. The glaze consists of an oily liquid sold in most paint stores. Called glazing liquid or glaze coat, it is a milky colorless oil. Tinting oil colors are used to color the glazing liquid. To make the mixing easier, first thin the tinting colors with tur-

pentine or mineral spirits. We used this basic recipe: One tablespoonful of color stirred into ¼ cup of thinner, then both added to ½ pint of glazing liquid. Stir vigorously.

The color will look a lot deeper in the container than it will when applied and rubbed off. Experiment on the test surface to determine the effect you want. Add more color if a more opaque or heavier glaze is de-

sired. The glaze coat dries slowly, so there is plenty of time to wipe and blend it. If the effect is not pleasing, you may wipe the glaze off completely with a rag moistened with paint thinner. Then brush the glaze on, one section at a time.

Brushing can be haphazard, but should be thorough. The entire surface should be covered without skipping. The glaze should be allowed

71

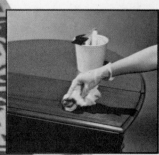

to set for about 5-10 minutes but is still workable up to ½ hour later.

Cheesecloth is most commonly used for wiping. For the pieces shown, however, we also used other materials to achieve a variety of finishes. For the china cabinet, we applied a white glaze over a darker base coat and rolled a wad of clear-plastic wrap across it to achieve a semi-marbleized effect.

For the chest of drawers, we applied a dark brown glaze over the yellow and white base coats and wiped with a plastic pot scrubber, softening the finish with a stiff-bristled basting brush.

For the rocker, we applied a yellow glaze over the orange base coat and wiped with rough-grade steel wool. For the end table, we applied a dark glaze over an ochre base coat and wiped with cheesecloth; we then spattered concentrated glaze color on with an old toothbrush. For the gate-leg table, we appled a blue glaze over the green base coat and wiped with fine-grade steel wool, then softened the effect with cheesecloth.

As you wipe, remember not to rub the glaze off uniformly. Allow more to remain in grooves and carvings while wiping most of the glaze off on the high spots. On flat surfaces, wipe off more in the center, leaving it darker around the edges.

3. For the final protective coat, use a clear, low-luster varnish. After the glaze coat has dried for at least a day or two, test the varnish in one corner to make sure it will not lift off or dissolve the glaze. On dresser tops, tabletops and other surfaces that get hard wear, it is best to wipe on a light coat of paste wax after the final coat of varnish has dried for several days.

72

Apartment Decorating

Apartments pose a special set of problems and challenges seldom encountered by people who live in houses. And that holds whether you live in the ordinary apartment, the garden variety, multiple family housing, or even in a condominium. Limited and confining space probably tops the list of grievances with off-center windows, awkward beams and protruding posts among other com-

Continued on page 75

With imaginative planning, a tiny, one-room studio can be as aesthetically stimulating and almost as livable as a whole house. Here, plaid carpeting wall-to-wall sets the pace and establishes the warm color scheme. The burgundy tones are repeated in the paint on walls and ceiling, and the black accents in shiny, mini-slat window blinds. A double bed, heaped with bolsters and toss pillows, doubles for sitting. Backed by a trio of campaign chests, it divides living space from dressing area. Self-stick mirror tiles on closet doors and a small portion of the opposite wall give the room the illusion of continuing on forever. Magic ingredient in the living area is a console chest that conceals an extension table. With a single leaf, the table becomes deck size. Storage trunks with latex foam cushions can be swung around for seating dinnner guests. Wall-hung shelves are painted to match the walls.

mon plights. Rooms seem to be either too small, too narrow, too few, or just plain dull architecturally. Storage space is minuscule. With imagination plus a little know-how and carefully thought-out planning, you can find solutions to these common apartment-decorating problems.

Who says a room has to be square and boxlike? Two small curved sections of silver-papered hardboard on either side of a spectacular wall graphic create the illusion of a semi-round room and make a perfect foil for mercury-bulb lighting. A curved sofa, round cocktail table and elliptical steel rocker accent the curviliner feeling. Bookcases house not only books and artifacts, but a bar and entertainment center as well. A mirrored wall in the dining "L" doubles the expanse of glass-top table, pendant lighting and floor-to-ceiling wall. Latticework screens, covered with silver Mylar, visually divide dining area from kitchen; vinyl flooring in both areas establishes continuity.

A platform literally sets the "L" apart from the rest of the room, at the same time providing extra seating and a stereo niche. One section lifts for storage and radiator access. A shelfful of plants makes additional window treatment totally unnecessary. Random bands of color painted on the wall free-hand (below) add vivid impact to the tiny dining area.

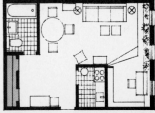

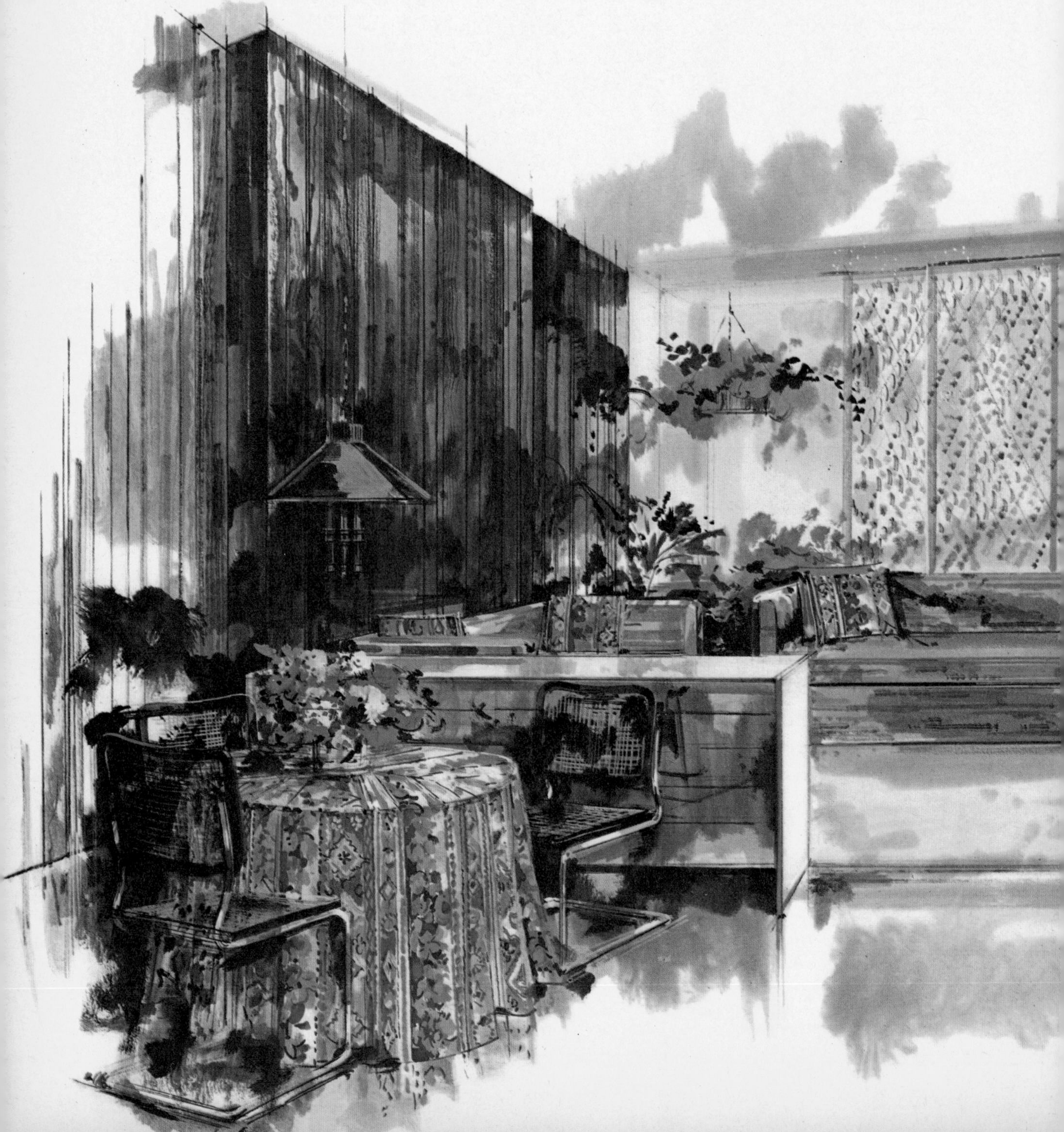

Most unique about this arrangement is the placement of furniture away from the walls. The reason: To take advantage of the one long wall for hideaway work space. A pair of 4'x8' wall panels slide apart to reveal a sewing and fix-it center behind. Pegboard organizes tools and sewing supplies. Similarly, filigree panels installed on sliding tracks two feet in front of the window wall create a garden spot for potted plants between. A swivel chair, love seat and convertible sofa-bed are upholstered to match, unifying the conversation area. A storage chest defines the dining "L" and doubles as a serving buffet. The round table is skirted to the floor with a tablecloth made from a sheet.

Sunny yellow window shades with shade cloth strips glued above and around dramatically transform problem windows and awkward beams into graphic art. The sofa, at right angle to the wall, creates a divide for the desk area behind. A sculptural lamp illuminates both desk and sofa. The Plexiglas cocktail table is on casters, so it easily rolls aside when the sofa is opened to a bed. A pair of old chests, freshly repainted, line up along the long wall to serve storage needs. Wall-to-wall carpeting and a small wall covered with self-adhesive mosaic mirror tiles help create the illusion of more space than there actually is.

Apartment Furnishing

Few of us expect to live in one home forever. Today mobility is the norm rather than the exception. An apartment is the first home for most couples just starting out. Usually, with the arrival of children comes a move to the first house. How does one meet the challenge of the recurring dilemma? With wise purchasing and a long-range plan, first-apartment furnishings can work equally as well in a future home. To prove our point, we first furnished a one-bedroom apartment in Denver (all photos along the top of these pages), then literally picked up and moved those furnishings into a three-bedroom Chicago townhouse (along the bottom of the pages). Notice especially how they frequently change in appearance and use, yet successfully coordinate with the necessary new acquisitions.

Our first apartment boasts of bright color, do-it-yourself touches and a minimum in the way of basic furniture to buy. Wicker chairs with plump cotton cushions, colorful, inexpensive crepe paper flowers and the old mason jars typify our early-marriage scheme. The same squat bottle, glass table and mason jars mature into sculptural sophistication in our next home (opposite). A diningroom table (above, right) becomes a desk in a future study/guest room (right); a pair of etageres, part of a wall of bookshelves. Cotton print draperies (right) were used in our first-apartment living room.

An in-total view of the apartment conversation area **(left)** reveals a sofa that is, in reality, a twin bed with a tailored cover. Head and footboard, end-to-end, plus toss pillows form a backrest. A wicker trunk is a store-all cocktail table and a place to display the wedding album. Wall-to-wall carpet and ceiling beams are included with this apartment. Another view of the house study/guest room **(below)** indicates where the rest of the living-room furnishings have gone. Our apartment bedroom **(opposite, top)** exemplifies the genius of many young couples on a budget. No-iron, cotton-blend sheets tailored to fit the bed and teamed with a pair of pillowcases negate the need for a spread. In place of a headboard: Sheet-clad 2x4s wedged between ceiling and floor. Also made from a sheet, the Roman shade plus tiebacks for the draperies that came with the apartment. The bent-chrome rocker might be considered a splurge, but it's a vital part of the next-home nursery **(opposite, below)**. You'll also recognize the canopy, table skirt, shutter curtains and crib cover made from the same sheeting. The campaign chests are perfect dressing-table height. The wicker etagere and one former living-room chair move into the master bedroom **(opposite, below)** along with the queen-size bedding. The rest of the furnishings, including brass headboard and bedspread, are new.

80

Step through the front door of any small apartment and chances are you're right in the middle of the living room. A modular shelf system establishes our apartment entryway **(left)** and divides conversation area from dining area. Bonus function: It solves our desk-space and storage problems. So the radio could face the living room without baring its back, we wallpapered it! In the next home, the desk unit again defines an entry **(below, left)**. The Chippendale dining chairs look equally respectable around a glass dining table **(below, right)** and, by adding a pair of matching armchairs **(one shown, opposite, below)**, we can now seat six. One good buy is worth repeating, so, along with our new home, we acquired a mate to the chrome sling chair, a second butcher-block-look plastic-laminate table and another smoked-glass lamp **(three photos below)**. The wall-hung rug, a Paul Klee limited edition and an admitted indulgence **(at right and directly below)**, is a focal point in both living rooms. Other new-home acquisitions include a pair of love seats upholstered in velour, a coffee table, cotton print draperies and sheet-vinyl flooring.

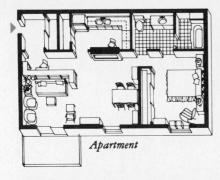

Apartment

House: First floor

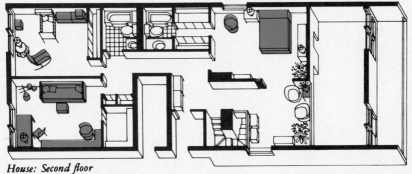

House: Second floor

The floor plans show disposition of furnishings from the one-bedroom apartment to the three-bedroom house. All furnishings shown in blue on the house plan came from the first apartment.

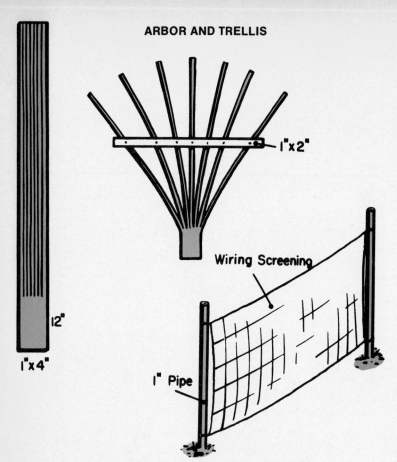

1"x2"

12"

1"x4"

Wiring Screening

1" Pipe

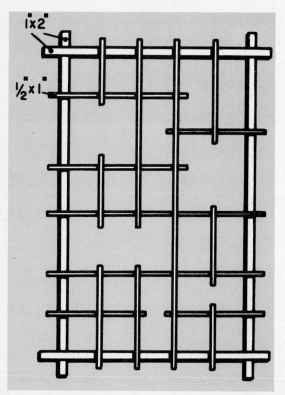

1"x2"

½"x1"

Arbor and Trellis

The terms "arbor" and "trellis" are generally used interchangeably; however, the former is the heavier archway structure under which people walk, whereas the trellis need be only a latticework of wood strips as a support for climbing plants.

Arbor

This must be strong enough to carry the weight of flowers and foliage which you train over the framework. The structure can be made simply by securely setting rows of tall wood posts into the ground, and nailing boards across them at the top. They may be straight across, or come to a point in the center or, if you want a rounded arch, use lightweight upright wood strips and bend them to form the arch. To secure them in place, nail horizontal strips across them at regularly-spaced intervals.

The upright sides of the arbor are also strengthened by nailing across horizontal strips, forming a crisscross, straight or diagonal pattern.

Use rustproof nails and outdoor paint to withstand the weather.

Trellis

This is usually built against a fence or the wall of the house or garage, and vines and other climbing plants are trained over the trellis. It is often constructed to stand on its own, without being supported by a wall.

The design of the trellis depends on your own taste, the space in your garden or backyard, the materials you use. Wood is most generally used. Upright strips are secured in the ground, and horizontal strips are nailed across, in crisscross, straight or diagonal pattern.

If the trellis is against the house or garage, paint the wood to match the color of the structure against which it rests; this gives an uncluttered appearance to the house exterior. Here, too, use outdoor paint and rustproof nails.

A trellis is sometimes made of rope or wire, stretched and nailed in a pattern against a fence or wall. This is not recommended for heavy vines, but it serves the purpose for lighter-weight plants. The rope or wire should be sturdy enough to withstand weather conditions.

6 Simple Trellises and Arbors

1. This fan-shaped trellis can be made in less than an hour. If you have a power saw, the whole job will take only a few minutes. All you need is a 6′ length of 1x4 and a 30″ piece of 1x2. It is best if you make the trellis out of redwood, which is weather-resistant and decay-proof. Just mark off ½″ intervals along the edge of the 1x4 and make parallel saw cuts as shown, leaving the bottom 12″ uncut. Then take the piece of 1x2 and nail the extended ½″

strips to it with two 3d aluminum nails into each strip. You can use rustproof screws if you wish in place of the nails.

2. Another very simple trellis can be made by sinking two 1″ diameter pipes into the earth. Sink about 18″ to 24″ and leave anywhere from 60″ to 72″ exposed above the ground level. Buy rustproof screening and attach it to each of the posts. You can wind a thin wire through the openings in the screening just as would be done when sewing. This makes an attractive trellis but can be used only for light-weight climbers. Do not use heavy vines unless you use "hardware cloth"—a heavy screening—between the two pipes. Most hardware stores sell hardware cloth screening with ½″ spaces.

3. A rectangular trellis with woven vertical and horizontal pieces can be built out of 1x2 lumber and ½x1 strips, both of which are readily available at any lumber yard. The

85

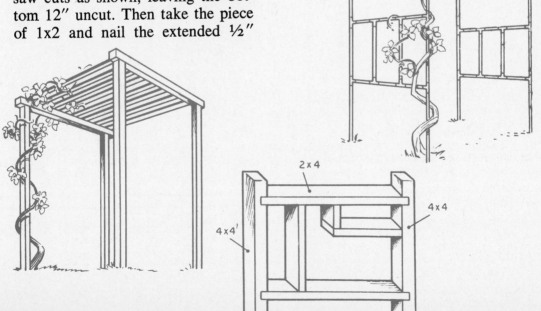

2 x 4

4 x 4′

4 x 4

two outside pieces and the top and bottom cross pieces of this trellis are made out of 1x2's held with two rust-proof screws at each joint. The other sections of the trellis are cut out of ½x1 strips and nailed in place with 2 aluminum nails at each joint. These strips can run the full length vertically and horizontally or can be attached in an open weave form as shown in this sketch.

4. If you have heavy vines or wish to have your trellis stand free, away from any additional support, such as a house or garage, make it out of heavier lumber. This free-form model is made out of 2x4's and 4x4's, preferably redwood. However, you can use cedar or cypress if either of these is more readily available. The two upright posts plus the top and base horizontal supports are made of 4x4's. The corners are jointed by cutting dado joints, or toe-nail the pieces in place. Cut pieces of 2x4 redwood for the inner members of this trellis and toe-nail in place with aluminum nails.

5. An easy-to-make arbor is built along the same lines as the heavy vine trellis. The uprights at each end are cut out of 4x4 redwood, cedar or cypress. If you use pine, coat the lumber with a wood preservative and paint with a quality outdoor paint. The top cross sections at each end are also cut out of 4x4 stock. The arbor should be at least 6' 6" high and a minimum of 40" wide. How far apart you set the two end posts depends upon the size you wish to make your arbor. If this distance is 5' or less, you can nail lattice strips across the top. If the space is 5' to 7' use 1x2 lumber.

6. Maybe you'd like to make your arbor out of craftworker's aluminum.

There are special fittings available in retail stores selling this aluminum which enable you to join the tubing stock. Use either 1" or 1¼" diameter tubing for the arbor. The corner joints are secured by using 90° elbows. The other joining of the tubing is done with T-butt connectors. You have an almost unlimited choice of designs from which to select. Plan your arbor by drawing it to scale on paper; then purchase the necessary parts and you will find that the entire job will take only a few hours to complete.

Architectual Symbols

If you like to make your own plans in fixing up your house, or if you want to know how to read blueprints, these symbols are used universally in the building trades.

Architectural Abbreviations

BRK	Brick
CI	Cast iron
CLG	Ceiling
CEM	Cement
CONC	Concrete
DR	Dining room
DHW	Double hung window
EXT	Exterior
FIN	Finish
FL	Floor
GI	Galvanized
GL	Glass
INT	Interior
K	Kitchen
LR	Living room
MC	Medicine chest
OC	On center
PLAS	Plaster
TC	Terra cotta
WI	Wrought iron

Building Construction

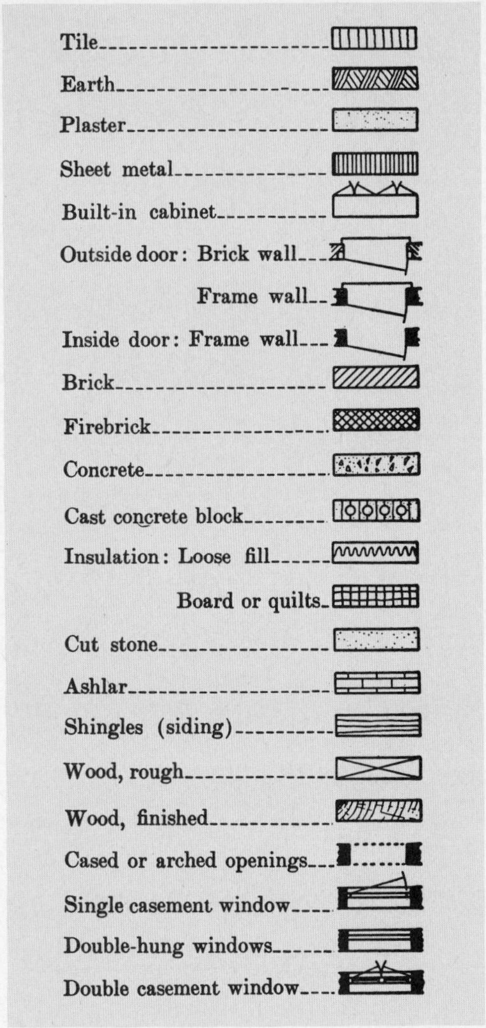

Tile
Earth
Plaster
Sheet metal
Built-in cabinet
Outside door: Brick wall
Frame wall
Inside door: Frame wall
Brick
Firebrick
Concrete
Cast concrete block
Insulation: Loose fill
Board or quilts
Cut stone
Ashlar
Shingles (siding)
Wood, rough
Wood, finished
Cased or arched openings
Single casement window
Double-hung windows
Double casement window

Grease trap
Hose bibb or sill cock
Lavatories:
    Pedestal
    Wall-hung
    Corner
Toilets:
    Tank
    Flush valve
Urinals:
    Stall-type
    Wall-hung
Laundry trays
Built-in shower
Shower
Sinks:
    Single drain board.
    Double drain board.

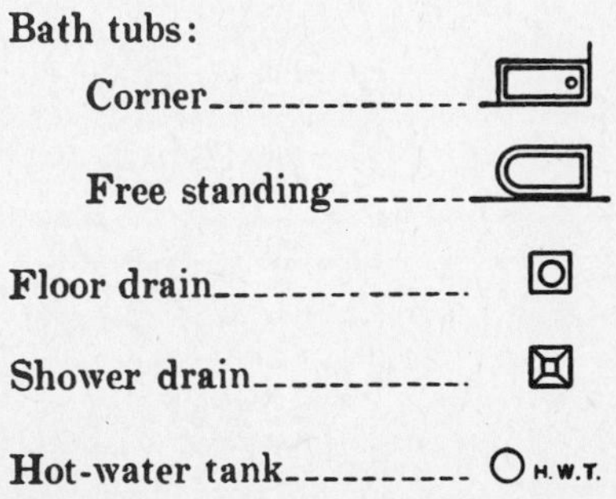

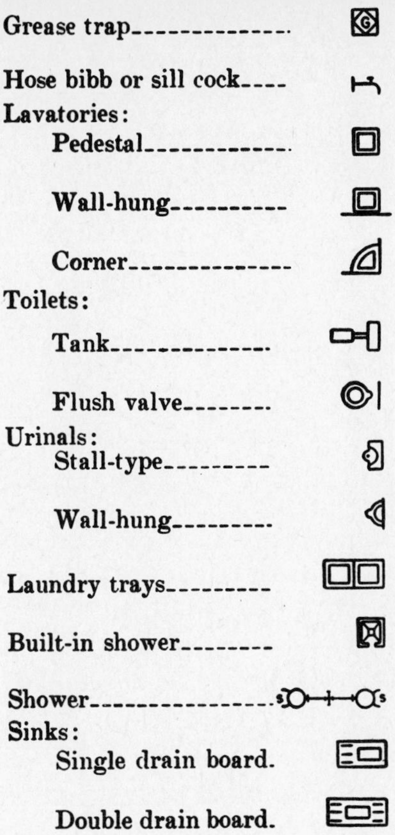

Heating, Ventilating and Appliance

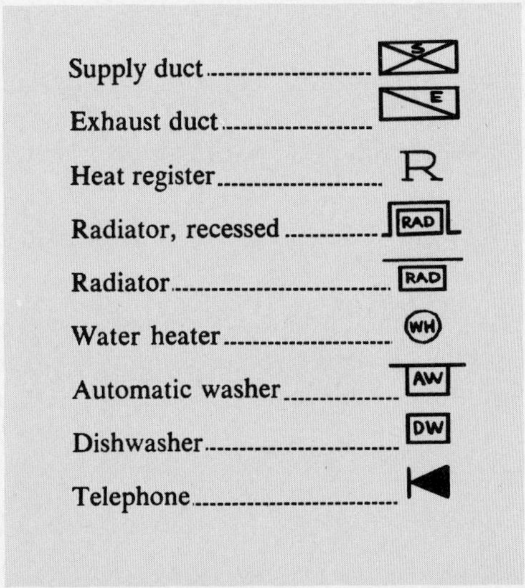

Supply duct
Exhaust duct
Heat register
Radiator, recessed
Radiator
Water heater
Automatic washer
Dishwasher
Telephone

Plumbing

Bath tubs:
    Corner
    Free standing
Floor drain
Shower drain
Hot-water tank

87

Electrical

Pull switch	●P.S.	Ceiling outlet		
Single-pole switch	S₁	Wall bracket		
Double-pole switch	S₂	Single convenience outlet		
Triple-pole switch	S₃	Double convenience outlet		
Buzzer		Ceiling outlet, gas & electric		
Floor outlet				
Bell		Motor		
Drop cord		Light outlet with wiring and switches indicated		

Archway

The large, open archway between two rooms, or leading from the hall, may be closed up if you desire. A pair of French doors could be hung inside the archway. Or, if you wish more wall space and a single door, the archway could have built-in shelves on either side, for books and ornaments, and the door hung in the center between the two rows of shelves.

If you don't want to close the arch-

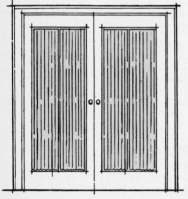

1. A pair of French doors can be set within a framework set into an arch between two rooms. If you wish, you can make your own door frames, using corrugated Fiberglas as the interior material within the door frame.

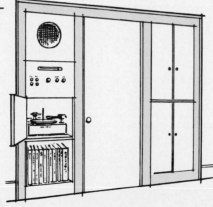

2. If there's a wide opening between the two rooms, you can put the space to use with a built-in. Here on the left wall is a Hi-Fi unit— tuner, phonograph and record storage, plus the speaker. Sliding cabinets provide storage of other items to the right of the door.

3. If you still want an open feeling but prefer a definite separation between the two rooms, follow this technique. Two base frames about 36″ to 48″ are made of plywood with trim molding added on the outside. Large columns are used to tie the base in with the ceiling.

Small corridor kitchen is made visually larger by removing door to dining room and enlarging the opening.

way permanently, but desire a temporary closing, a wide folding screen or a pair of screens will fulfill that function adequately. The screens could be covered decoratively, or painted a solid color to match the wall.

4. Round archways present more of a problem but here too the problem is easily solved. Toe-nail a double 2 x 4 across the top of the opening to make a square frame for folding doors. Use panels of opaque glass set in wood trim molding to fill in the top.

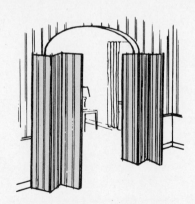

5. Decorative screens, finished in a wallpaper to match that on the walls, can be used to seal one room off from the other. If you want that open feeling at times, just move the screens aside. Screens are easily made out of 2 x 2 lumber and plywood.

89

Attics

Converting an attic to greater usefulness is a project that anyone can undertake without too much trouble using the basic handyman tools. The starting point in the conversion project is to clean out the attic. Sift through the things which you have accumulated there. Probably many of these items can be used and put to work in the project. The next step, and the hardest, is to throw out the items that cannot be used. Remember that in your construction you will be able to make room for limited storage space under the eaves. After you have put in the partitions to convert the majority of the floor area into rooms you will need, you can plan the under-eaves storage space for a variety of items in drawers and on shelves.

A typical attic conversion will require the various tools and materials which are listed. You won't need all of this material immediately if you plan to finish your attic in easy stages and do a room at a time. This list is your starting point but the exact amount of equipment and material you use will be determined by the size of your project and the amount of work you plan to do yourself.

Hints and Suggestions on Attic Planning and Construction

1. Check with your lumber yard and building supply dealer for his advice and valuable tips. Show him your rough sketch. He can suggest material which is practical, easy to handle and inexpensive.

2. Plan your attic bathroom or plumbing installation so that it is above the other bathroom in the main portion of the house to simplify installation work and reduce the amount of pipe necessary for the conversion project.

3. Check into the various finance plans wth easy payments offered by some lumber yards for home repairs and remodeling.

4. To cut costs, make your own doors of 1x4 lumber frames which are then sandwiched between hardboard, plywood or other decorative material. For a decorative touch, use brass headed upholstery nails to form various patterns and designs.

5. During the pencil and paper stage of your attic planning try to include as many built-in features as possible. These can be used for storage, furniture, work surfaces and seating arrangements. You will find

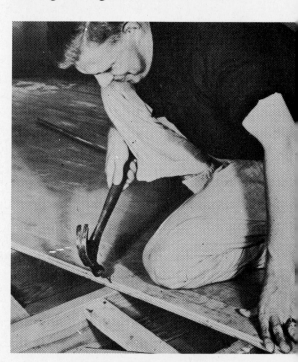

Photograph courtesy Owens-Corning Fiberglas Corp.

Install a subfloor so that you can work and move around without crashing through the ceiling of the room below. This installation is of tongue-and-groove flooring. Plywood sheets can also be used.

90

This attic was turned into bad-weather play space with a minimum of architectural change. It can also sleep up to four guests in cozy bunks (two tucked under each eave) framed in rough-sawed plywood siding.

that designing and building these features will save you money on furnishings for the new space.

6. Collect the pamphlets brochures and material supplied by the manufacturers to lumber yards and magazines to help you in your planning construction.

7. Prevent possible cold drafts by packing insulation around window frames and sills.

8. To lay out angular cuts for boards and any of the wall material which are to fit under eaves, measure the height from the floor at two points the width of the piece apart, mark them on the board or wall material and draw a straight line between these two points.

9. Secure the services of a qualified heating contractor to install the extensions from your existing heating plant.

10. Sound-deadening felt may be placed between the finished flooring and the subfloor for good inexpensive noise control.

Glossary of Attic Construction Terms

FRAMING—2 x 4's, 2 x 3's, etc., are dimensions of lumber for supporting the material which is used to form partitions and walls.

FURRING—Strips of wood, usually 1 x 2 or 1 x 3, applied to wall, ceiling or other surface to even it. Furring strips also provide an air space and form a base for the application of various types of wall coverings.

HEADER—A horizontal member

91

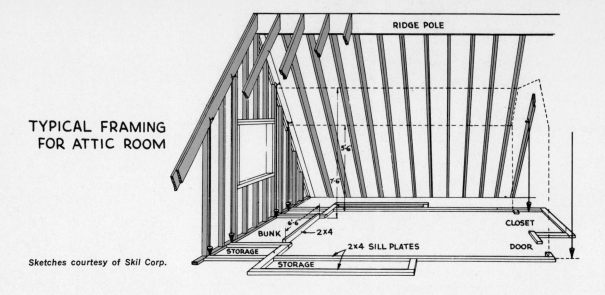

TYPICAL FRAMING
FOR ATTIC ROOM

Sketches courtesy of Skil Corp.

between the studs over window and door openings. Usually the same dimensions as the stud lumber.

JAMB—This term includes the sides of door and window openings.

JOIST—A horizontal supporting member to which the floor and ceiling are fastened.

KNEE-WALL—A low partition for the wall formed by the studs running from the sloping ceiling rafters to the floor or base plates.

PARTITION—A dividing wall within any story of the building.

PLATE—This term defines the horizontal member placed at the top (top plate) and at the bottom (sole plate) of studs. It is nailed into position to form the wall or partition.

PLUMB—Means that the material or lumber is in a perfectly vertical position.

RAFTER—The structural member, generally sloping, of a roof.

RIDGE—The highest horizontal member of a roof to which the upper ends of the rafters are fastened.

SHIM—The term used to refer to

building up behind furring or other construction member. It provides a solid backing and a true flush surface. Shimming is usually done with a wedge shaped piece of wood.

STUD—A vertical member in a wall or partition.

TOENAIL—To drive nails into a surface at an angle.

BASEBOARD—The wood trim at the bottom of the wall next to the floor.

BASE SHOE—A wood molding over the joint formed by the baseboard and the finished floor.

CLINCH—To drive nails through the lumber and bend the extended points back into the wood.

O.C.—On centers (from center to center i.e., 16″ on center).

Tools

The following are the basic tools necessary for framing and partitioning the attic: Hammer, saw, screw driver, carpenter's level, square, rule and some wooden horses or a short ladder.

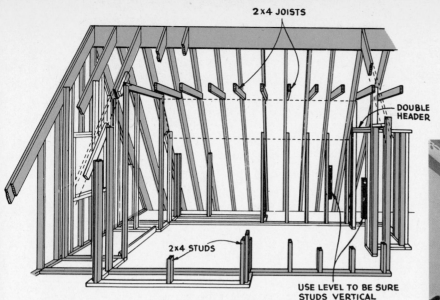

2X4 JOISTS

DOUBLE HEADER

2X4 STUDS

USE LEVEL TO BE SURE STUDS VERTICAL

This attic bedroom is a decorative gem, with pebble-pattern vinyl floor below, painted beams and daisy-stenciled ceiling above, and great style in-between.

Construction Materials Needed

1. 2x3 or 2x4 framing lumber
2. 1x2 furring strips (for plank-type finishes)
3. Fiberglas, wool, batt, or granule insulation
4. Nails (several sizes)
5. Wall finish (plywood, gypsum, composition board)
6. Floor covering (linoleum, tile, carpeting)
7. Wood trim (moldings of various kinds)
8. Sub-flooring lumber
9. Flooring lumber
10. Flooring underlayment and felt
11. Mastic (for floor tile)
12. Doors
13. Windows or dormers
14. Plaster and lath (optional)
15. Heating equipment
16. Electrical wiring, lighting, outlets, switches
17. Plumbing connections
18. Custom made built-ins
19. Wallpaper
20. Paint
21. Hardware and fixtures
22. Window glass, mirrors, etc.
23. Ceiling material, board or tiles

How To Plan

It is always better to work with paper and pencil. If you can get a plan of your house from the builder use it as a guide. Measure floor space in the attic and make a scale drawing using 1″ to represent 1′. The division of the attic space depends upon your personal needs as well as the final use of the space. There is virtually an unlimited number of layouts you can plan for the attic conversion. Manu-

93

Collar beams or ceiling joists are installed at a minimum height of 7½'. They may be cut from 2x4s and nailed to the rafters.

facturers of building materials and lumber dealers can supply you with pamphlets and brochures suggesting various layouts and designs for attic bedrooms, apartments, dens and living rooms. Custom made built-ins, also described and illustrated in the brochures, should be provided for and can be tailored to the space requirements. Study a number of these dealer suggestions to see which are suited to your physical needs, your financial abilities and your craftsmanship. Don't cut a board or hammer a nail until you have set down on paper a plan of operation and a general plan of the floor plan of the attic. When you have reached this point in your preparations it is a good idea to visit your lumber dealer with your plans and specifications. He can advise you about the types and advantages of the material you will need, give you building tips and can tell you what specific tools you will need.

Proceed in an organized fashion to finish your attic. In this way you will make the job easier, will keep a check on your progress and will avoid costly and time-consuming mistakes. The following steps are suggested as a guide and checklist:

1. Check the attic for electrical, heating and plumbing lines. If none have been provided, they are your major and first consideration.

2. If no subfloor has been installed or you have a walk down the center, lay the subfloor.

3. For more headroom and light, install a gable or shed dormer.

4. Nail knee-wall studs and ceiling joists, called collar beams.

5. Locate and erect partition walls to separate one room from another and make door frames.

6. Install the wiring for fixtures, switches and outlets, or have contractor do so if local building code requires it.

7. If you are adding a bathroom to the attic, have plumbing lines installed according to local code requirements.

8. Choose your insulation and in-

Partition studs are installed after the new wall and ceiling are placed. 2 x 4's are used and the partitions may be assembled on the floor then raised into place.

Make sure you provide for lighting, wiring, and plumbing. Check local building codes concerning these installations; it may be required to have such work done by licensed electricians or plumbers.

Photographs courtesy of Owens-Corning Fiberglas Corp.

stall according to manufacturers' instructions.

9. Install the ceiling and wall materials.

10. Add selected finish floor over attic subfloor.

11. Install decorative trim to cover floor, wall and ceiling joints. Add trim around windows and doors.

12. Design built-ins and install them in the finished rooms.

13. Paint, wallpaper and finish ceiling, wall surfaces, built-ins and woodwork.

14. Install light fixtures, wall switches and wall outlets.

15. Move in furnishings and equipment.

Basic Framing For Attic Walls and Ceilings

The basic framing of an attic is comprised of the following steps:

1. Laying of the subfloor if the joists are exposed.

2. Join sloping roof with floor by erecting knee-walls.

3. Locate and install collar beams to form frame for ceiling.

4. Lay out and construct partition walls to divide attic into rooms.

Install the Subfloor

Installation of the subfloor will permit you to work and move about freely without danger of crashing through the ceiling of the room below. There are two types of subflooring you can install. One is tongue-and-groove flooring, which is rough sheathing lumber installed on the diagonal across the joists. The second is the ¾″ subfloor plywood. The plywood is much easier to install and saves a considerable amount of time. Nail the 4x8 plywood panels across the joists with 8-penny flooring nails, spaced 8″ apart.

Erecting the Knee-Walls

The minimum height advisable for knee-walls is at least 4′. Make sure that you provide for this height when you are locating the position for the floor plates. The knee-wall studs to form the attic side walls are attached to a base (floor) plate and the rafters. The base plate lumber should be the same dimension as the studs.

a. Line the base plate up to form lower edge of wall; nail through the subfloor into joists below with 16-penny nails.

b. Measure height of knee-wall stud from the base plate to the rafter above and cut studs to size, allowing one for each rafter.

c. Toe-nail stud to base plate with 8-penny nails and nail to side of rafters. Use a carpenter's level to make certain that studs are level.

To save time in checking level, erect first and last studs, check with level and stretch taut string between the two studs, using the string as guides to placement of other studs in the line.

When installing the knee-walls you may want to save some of the under-eaves space for storage; in this case do not attach studs in the storage areas. Frame this area by attaching a plate, the same size lumber as the studs, between the two studs forming the outside of the storage area.

Check the rafter spacing. Nearly

96

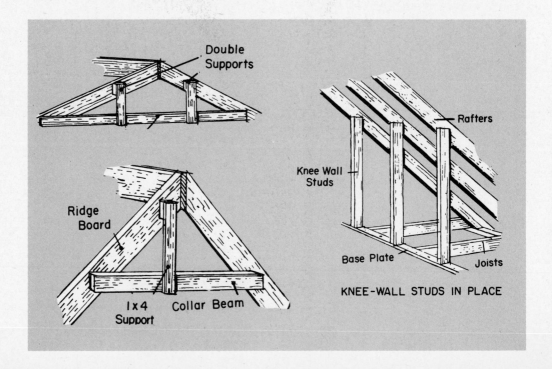

Double Supports

Ridge Board

1 x 4 Support

Collar Beam

Rafters

Knee Wall Studs

Base Plate

Joists

KNEE-WALL STUDS IN PLACE

all roof rafters are spaced on 16″, 20″ or 24″ centers to take advantage of the standard widths of blanket insulation. This spacing determines the space between the knee-wall 2x4's. If your rafters are not regularly spaced you may have to erect "false" rafters or cut insulation blankets to fit.

Installing the Collar Beams

Many building codes specify that the bottom of the ceiling joist shall be a minimum of 7′6″ from the floor. Since it is difficult to install a ceiling at an angle, collar beams or ceiling joists are added.

If the ceiling joists are less than 6′ long use 2x3's. For wider ceilings, use 2x4's and secure these joists to the rafters with 16-penny nails. Use a single nail to tack one end of the 2x4 in place at the correct height, level, and attach to the rafter at the other side with a single nail. Now, mark the length for cutting and use this piece as a pattern to cut the rest of your ceiling joists.

It is not necessary to add an extra support to hold the joist in narrow attics, if your ceiling joist is over 8′ long, then use a 1x4 nailed to the joist as close to the ridge board as possible. On a 12′ ceiling joist use a double support—one on each side of the ridge board.

You will need ventilation over your insulation for vapor control and summer comfort. Provide now in your construction for a vent at either end of your house.

Decide on the final ceiling finish now, while you are installing the ceiling framing. If you are going to use large boards to finish the ceiling you will have to make provisions for nailing boards. This means you should

Once an unused attic, this area now serves as playroom, guest room, and bedroom for two boys. Built-ins are used extensively to make the best use of available space. Skylight windows in the red cedar ceiling bring sun and size into the rooms.

97

insert 2x3 or 2x4 lumber at each place where the edges of the sheet must be nailed, including corners. If a vertical plank type finish is to be installed, furring strips, described later, will be needed.

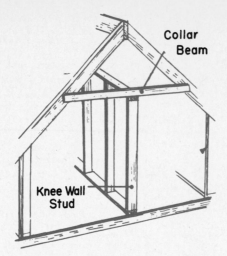

PARTITION WALL IN THE ATTIC

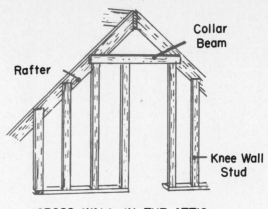

CROSS WALL IN THE ATTIC

Fiberglas roll blanket insulation may be installed as shown at left. Blanket insulation may be nailed or stapled between the wall studs and ceiling joists.

Installing Frame Partitions

If you have included separate rooms with partitions to divide them in your planning this is the next step in your project. The partition walls can be built to run parallel or at right angles to the center ridge board. Use the same size lumber, 2x3's or 2x4's, for the wall studs. Walls that run the length of the attic, parallel to the center ridge board, require a top plate as well as the floor plate.

Cut a 2x4 base plate and partition studs to the proper length, allowing for a top plate to be added later. You can prefabricate your wall partition on the floor of the attic. Tip up your prefabricated assembly in place and nail the base plate to the floor. Make your top plate for the partition, attach it to the rafters and nail through it into the top of the vertical partition studs. Built-ins which you have planned should be installed at this time. Be sure to make provisions for the door framing.

Framing a Doorway

Do not install a floor plate in the door frame openings. To determine the proper size for the opening, select your door and check its dimensions. The overall width of the doorway is the width of the door itself plus 4¾" to allow for the extra studs and the finished jamb around the door. The overall height is the height of the door plus 1" if you do not plan to use a threshold, or 2" if you do.

Lighting and Plumbing

Before any more carpentry is done in the attic, now is the time to provide for lighting and plumbing. Local building codes may require that this work be done by an electrician or a plumber.

Before

An attic apartment is a project which can be undertaken inexpensively and take care of the immediate housing needs of the newlyweds or a place for the in-laws.

After

For wiring details and plumbing techniques and information, see *LIGHTING, WIRING* and *PLUMBING.*

Insulation

Insulating the attic living space is essential not only for added warmth in the winter but to keep out the sun's heat in summer. Three major areas must be insulated for proper efficiency: The floor between the knee-walls and the outside of the house, the end walls, knee-walls and the sloping rafter walls and over the ceiling. You must use an adequate thickness of insulation to keep the rooms comfortable at all times.

There are a number of types of insulating material available: Fiberglas batts or blankets, granule insulation, expandable aluminum foil and others. Follow the manufacturers' instructions for proper installation.

Also see *INSULATION.*

Finishing the Interior

There is a wide variety of attractive and easy-to-install wall materials available. If you plan to use the vertical plank type finish you will have to install 1x2 horizontal furring strips spaced 12″ to 16″ apart. Nail these strips to the studs or joists on all wall and ceiling areas. Be sure to provide a nailing surface on both sides of all angles and corners.

If you decide to use any of the large wallboard materials your job will be easier and faster. Listed here are a number of the materials available and their characteristics.

WALLBOARD (CANE AND FIBRE)—A moderately durable wall surfacing material. Some types come already prefinished. They have good insulating qualities and are moderately soundproof.

WALLBOARD (PRESSED WOOD)—Tough surface is difficult to damage. Made in various finishes and patterns, including perforated and corrugated. Easily painted and moderately priced.

WALLBOARD (PLASTER OR ASBESTOS) — Fire-resistant surfaces. Moderately durable and low in cost. Flat dull surface needs painting or papering. Some now available in simulated wood grains.

PLYWOOD—Strong, with the surface available in different grains and wood species and surface finishes. Takes a permanent finish nicely

99

and is easily installed. Comes in both panels and planks.

PLASTIC-SURFACED HARD-BOARD)—These prefinished surfaces come in all colors and are easily cleaned. Also available in wood grains and marble effects. Durable surface and moderately priced. Most new types fasten to wall with special concealed hardware and clips or adhesives.

LINOLEUM, VINYL AND RUBBER—Available in rolls of various widths and tiles, Applied to solid wall surfaces with various adhesives. Can

The finished project will give you an extra attractive room like the one shown above. An attic project is low in cost and long on satisfaction.

Photograph courtesy makers of Armstrong's Temlock

Furring strips must be installed if you plan to use a vertical plank type wall finish. The strips are nailed to studs and joists on all wall and ceiling areas to provide nailing members.

Photograph courtesy Owens-Corning Fiberglas Corp.

Large sheets of wallboard or paneling go up quickly to cover walls and ceiling.

Photograph courtesy U.S. Plywood Corp.

Laying a tile floor in the attic.

Photographs courtesy Bakelite Co.

101

be applied to plasterboard and hardboard. Great variety of colors, designs and textures. Easy to maintain and moderately priced.

CORK—Manufactured in tiles 12″ x 12″ or 12″ x 24″. Glued to solid walls or comes already backed on hardboard. Moderately high priced. Good insulator and sound absorber but unless treated, stains easily.

LUMBER—Individual boards and planks, random or selected widths, available in different grains and species. Easily nailed to framing; can be given a permanent natural finish to highlight grain.

The technique used to apply the wall surfacing depends upon the material you have chosen to finish the interior. To install the plank type finish just mentioned after you have

What was once a dismal, empty garret has been transformed into a lovely guest room, as if by magic. Ceiling tile and false beams give the room a classic look that welcomes visitors.

Photo courtesy Conwed Corporation

nailed up the furring strips, regular or random width 1″ stock boards are nailed with edges butting; use 8-penny finishing or casing nails to attach the planks to ceiling and floor plates, studs and braces. Use a nail set to sink heads of nails below surface. Fill nail holes.

CEMENTING PLYWOOD—Plywood panels, ¼″ thick, are secured with 1½″ long finishing nails into the plates, studs and braces. One of the latest methods of applying plywood walls is with contact cement. The plywood is cemented to the studs, so there is no countersinking nail heads and filling in nail holes be-fore finishing. If you work two sides of the wall at one time there will be no time lost in waiting for the special cement to harden.

The following lists the steps and method of cementing your wall in place:

1. Measure and cut panel to exact size, then lay panel in place and mark location of the studs. When additional panels are to be added the plywood comes to the center of the stud.

2. Work on the reverse side of the plywood and use a straight edge to rule a line corresponding to the center of the studs marked off.

3. Brush an adhesive such as

Weldwood Contact Cement over the lines to line up with location of studs. Apply cement liberally.

4. Using the same method, apply cement to the studs. Cement must set for thirty minutes to two hours; on sloping surfaces apply a second coat of the contact cement.

5. Panel is placed in position. With sloping wall installation you will need assistance.

6. Do not apply any pressure initially, so that you can shift panel slightly to get it perfectly aligned. When properly placed, secure by using hammer and wood block to set cement. The wood block will prevent damage and marks to your panel.

SECURING OTHER WALL SURFACES—Hardboard panels are best secured with 1″ flathead sheet metal screws through pre-drilled holes spaced 8″ apart. Pre-finished hardboard planks and tiles, interlock with tongue-and-groove joints and are held by special metal clips supplied by the manufacturer.

Wallboard can be applied in several different ways. If the surface is to be painted or wallpapered, use 6-penny coated common nails. The new pre-finished panels are also attached with special clips or with 6-penny casing nails set 6″ to 8″ apart.

Linoleum, plastic and rubber tiles must be cemented to the wall. A sub-grade of plywood or plaster-board is attached to the studs and braces with nails, setting the nails flush with the surface and cementing the tiles over the rigid wall surface.

CEILING FINISHING—A variety of finishes is available for the ceiling. Depending upon the material you have used for the walls, you may want to cover the ceiling with the same material. The instructions for using the material are basic and the same techniques should be applied. On the other hand, you may wish to use a ceiling tile which is available in a number of textures and materials. The installation of tiles for the ceiling is a job that you can tackle

103

Photograph courtesy Wood Conversion Co.

Photograph courtesy U.S. Plywood Corp.

Ceiling tiles may be installed over furring strips or directly to an existing ceiling.

by yourself and you can work quickly and efficiently.

The first step in your job will be to square off the room. No matter how careful you were in your framing and wall covering, your ceiling is probably crooked. It will be your task to make the lines formed by the tiles seem square to the casual observer. To do this:

1. Find the center of the room by running a line diagonally across the room from one corner to another and then another line from the other corners of the room.

2. Using a protractor or angle divider, find the center of the angle formed by these diagonals and draw a line across the center of the room.

3. With a framing square draw a line at right angles to the line just drawn.

4. Determine how tiles will come out at the edges by dividing the distance from the center to the wall. Plan placement of the tiles so you do not have narrow edges on both sides of the wall.

To apply the tiles it is necessary to nail 1x3 furring strips at right angles to the ceiling joists with 6-penny common nails. The strips should be nailed 12" center to center for 12" tiles or 8" apart for 16" tiles. To secure the best results start the tiles at the center of the room and finish one row before you start another.

104

HINTS FOR HANDLING CEILING TILES:

1. For stapling or nailing, put fastener in each flange corner plus 1 staple or nail on flange side of 12" tiles or two for 16" tiles.

2. When starting tiles in center of the room, use a nailing strip (T shaped to fit grooves of tiles) or special clips, both available at lumber yards.

3. Attach first row of tiles from wall to wall. Each succeeding row is added from wall to wall before starting on the next row.

4. Score tiles several times with sharp knife or tile cutter on finished side, place over edge of table and snap off sharp edge. Tiles can also be cut with a saw; be sure to keep finished side up.

5. For a neater finish at edges where ceiling tiles meet wall, use a crown moulding. Use a trim to cover tiles brought down to kneewall.

FINISHING THE ATTIC FLOOR—In finishing your attic floor, once again you have a wide variety of materials to choose from. You can install a hardwood floor, linoleum or floor tile, wall to wall carpeting or any one of a dozen other materials depending upon what the rooms are designed for.

Hardwood finish flooring is installed in the same fashion as the tongue and groove subfloor. Never attempt to drive the nails all the way with the hammer. You will break the tongue. Use your nail set to drive the nail the last fraction of an inch. Finish the floor by sanding, staining and varnishing.

Linoleum is installed over a hardboard or plywood underlayment for a smooth finish. If your linoleum is felt-backed you can eliminate the felt padding. Cut the linoleum to fit, apply cement to the floor a few square feet at a time and press linoleum down into the cement. Follow the manufacturers' instructions.

To tile the floor, follow the same procedures for squaring the room as described in Tiling the Ceiling.

Room at the top for a growing girl has walls and ceiling covered with self-adhesive fabric. A wooden curtain rod sawed in half forms the frame for the bed canopy.

The following hints will aid you in doing a professional job.

1. Holes or openings between seams of plywood or subfloor should be filled.

2. Use an underlayment of felt paper base over the floor so that the joints in the subfloor or plywood will not show through.

3. Cut vinyl and rubber tiles with a sharp knife along a straight edge or use a powered jig saw. To cut asphalt tiles to size, score along line with sharp knife; repeat and then snap back from scored line.

4. Eliminate possibilities for error by cutting cardboard patterns for tiles being cut to fit irregular spaces.

5. Tiles should be kept at a 75 degree temperature. For best results warm tiles before laying. The tiles can be warmed near a furnace or heat carefully, using a blowtorch on asphalt tiles.

6. Apply adhesive with a toothed trowel. Flooring paper must show through grooves in the adhesive. After the adhesive has dried for an hour, remark chalk guide lines.

7. The first tile is set on the center of the cross line. Press tight and be careful to use *no* sliding motion.

8. Lay tiles fan-wise over one quarter of the room at a time. Lay all of the tiles in each of the sections except for the section butting against the wall. Follow the manufacturers pattern or design one of your own.

9. Leave ⅛″ for expansion space when you cut the tiles to fit against the baseboard.

ADDING WOOD TRIM—During the course of your carpentry in the attic you have probably made

105

more than a few unsightly joints and made other mistakes here and there. This is where your wood trim serves a dual purpose. While it will add a decorative touch to your project it will also conceal the mistakes. There are a variety of mouldings to choose from and your local lumber dealer will probably have many samples from which you can choose those you prefer.

DOOR TRIM—You can probably buy the lumber needed for door framing as a unit at your local lumber yard or purchase the individual moldings. The head jamb is nailed to the header over the door with 8-penny finishing nails. Next attach the side jambs in the same way. These should be 1″ stock boards cut wide enough to cover the edges of the wall material. The next step is to nail the casing, usually 1x4, with mitred corners to jamb and through wall studs so that 3/16″ of jamb is exposed. Attach the door to the jamb and finish by nailing a door stop along the sides and top with 6-penny finishing nails.

JOINT TRIM—A trim molding is needed to conceal the openings where the ceiling and walls meet and at the junction of walls and floor. It may also be necessary to use a trim molding at the point where the knee-wall ends. The types of molding and their locations are:

1. A crown molding, available in many sizes and styles is used to cover the ceiling-wall joint. Attach with 8-penny finishing nails into studs.

Small attic bath becomes a flower bower with walls and ceiling covered by bright plastic-coated wallpaper.

2. Baseboard at the wall-floor joint. This is usually three separate moldings. The baseboard is nailed to the studs with 8-penny finishing nails. A base mold is nailed to the top of that with 6-penny finishing nails. Then for a tight seal along the floor, a shoe mold is used. Window trims are provided with the stock windows purchased.

PAINTING AND DECORATING—Your last step is painting and decorating. Many finish boards do not require paint; if you used any of the pre-finish materials your work has been cut down quite a bit. Paint or stain the trim, depending upon your over-all decorating scheme. Curtains, furniture, lamps and rugs and other incidentals are now ready to be moved in.

Also see *PAINTING* and *WALL-PAPERING*.

STORAGE AREAS—If you had planned on under-eaves storage space here are some hints and suggestions which might prove useful in your planning. There are generally two ways to handle the unusual storage space provided by the under-eaves. One is a corner closet and the other is shallow storage units.

The corner areas adjoining a shed dormer are difficult to incorporate as

Before

A girl's room for study and entertainment was constructed in this attic where formerly leftovers and broken furniture took up valuable space.

After

107

FRAMING FOR A BUILT-IN

part of your attic living space. In this space you can readily make a side or front entrance closet for clothing or storage. Whether you decide to make a front entrance or side entrance closet, it will be necessary to:

1. Frame around the perimeter, constructing studs as you would normally do for partition walls.

2. A double stud must be erected on both sides of the door opening and a double header fits across the top of the opening. In the case of the side opening closet the header is cut at an angle to match the slope of the rafter.

3. Use a solid core flush door cut to size for the side entrance closet, or make one from 1x3's sandwiched between two pieces of ¼″ plywood.

4. The door is attached with hinges and a door pull and catch or any standard door hardware.

5. The front entrance closet door can be made in the same manner as the side entrance closet or use ¾″ plywood.

6. Attach closet hardware such as poles, hooks, racks or other, depending upon the items to be stored.

Shallow storage units are espe-

108

cially suitable for attics with low knee-walls and shallow under the eaves storage space. You can construct the storage space with sliding doors or open shelves or even drawers built into the walls.

The following steps will help you organize and work out your project.

1. After you have decided where and what type of built-in you need, leave an opening in the knee-wall and do not set any studs in place. Cut two short studs and attach them to the rafter and a floor plate at the rear of the storage space. They will form the other three sides of your built-in.

2. Across the rafters in this space add any wall surfacing material to seal off the built-in from side to side and from the front edge of the unit to the short studs in the back.

3. A quick, easy way to add shelf space, if it is to be covered with sliding doors, is to build a framed unit of ⅜″ or ½″ plywood. The shelves are attached by #8 flathead screws and the back is formed of hardboard or plywood. This unit is slid into place and a front baseboard is attached, if the unit is to be left open.

4. If you plan to conceal the unit behind sliding doors, make the entire unit as described but make it 1½″ less than the depth of the under-eaves closet to allow for the doors and track.

5. You can also turn the open shelves into drawers. Make the basic frame as described and drawers to fit into this. Follow the proportions suggested here for ease of handling and appearance.

a. If the drawer is less than 4 inches deep it can be made up to 18″ wide.

b. If the drawer is between 4″ and

7″ deep, the maximum width should be no more than 14″.

c. If the drawer is up to 12″ deep, make it no more than 12″ wide.

6. From ½″ plywood cut two sides and the front and back panels. Join these pieces with #6 flathead screws 1¼″ long, countersinking heads. Space these screws at least 3″ apart, using three to each corner.

7. Cut ½″x½″ cleats to fit inside this frame flush with the bottom edge. Hold the cleats to the sides with #6 flathead screws ¾″ long, spaced 2″ apart with countersunk heads.

8. The bottom of the drawer fits inside this frame and rests on the cleats. Cut the drawer bottoms from ¼″ plywood; secure with brads.

9. Faceplate of drawers, made of ¾″ plywood, is cut to extend ¼″ on all sides.

10. Secure the face plate to front panel by screws from inside of drawer. Use #6 flathead screws 1″ long spaced about 4″ apart along the top and bottom. Countersink heads.

CLOSETS IN THE ATTIC—

While on the subject of attic storage space you may want to consider dividing the attic with closet walls. You can make the walls functional by turning them into closets and the use of sliding doors will also save you valuable space. Constructing a closet wall begins in the same manner as erecting a wall. Plates and studs are nailed in position with an opening left for doors.

1. First complete the basic framing, then cut two studs to door height plus depth of sliding door hardware plus an additional ½″ for clearance.

After

Before

Wasted attic space becomes a cozy retreat for a teenaged girl. Wallpaper is accented by white-painted 1x4s, while poster bed is improvised from 4x4s wedged between floor and ceiling, supporting a plywood platform for box spring and mattress.

Gambrel roof and front dormers of this house allow several spacious and sunny rooms on the second floor. A red-felt-covered wall frames the windows of the dormer in one bedroom, with an accessoried window seat topping a storage bin. Another room—a tiny study—glows with earth tones in fabrics, woods, artifacts and other accessories (photo opposite page).

2. Nail these two studs to both sides of the opening with 10-penny nails. Cut a door header from two pieces of lumber, same dimensions as studs, long enough to rest on studs cut in previous step.

3. Nail both pieces together and toe-nail in place resting on studs.

4. If you make two closets back-to-back, add a divider wall between them of hardboard or utility grade plywood.

5. Add shelves to suit and clothes pole. The clothes pole, a 1½" or 2" dowel or metal rod, should be at least 63" above the floor for adults and about 45" for children.

6. Mount the sliding door hardware on the underside of the door header.

7. Buy two doors or make them from ¾" plywood or Novoply allowing 1" overlap in the center and about ¼" clearance above the floor plate.

8. Secure hardware to the doors and lift into place. The wall surfacing material is applied over framing and exposed surfaces and decorative trim is added around the door and joints.

Also see *BUILT-INS*.

ADDING A DORMER—If your attic ceiling is so low that you cannot make efficient use of the attic space

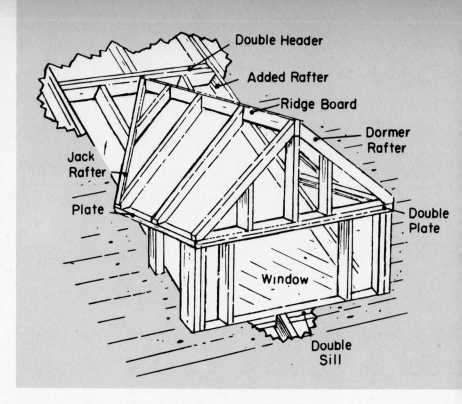

Double Header

Added Rafter

Ridge Board

Dormer Rafter

Jack Rafter

Plate

Double Plate

Window

Double Sill

the chances are that you will have to raise the ceiling of the attic by constructing a dormer. The two types of dormers most commonly used are gable and shed. A gable dormer usually provides only one window and is generally constructed in attics which have sufficient headroom but little light. A shed dormer raises the entire roof line of a house except at the ridge.

Building a dormer is the hardest part of reconverting an attic and you may want to hire a professional carpenter. If, however, you feel that you can tackle a project such as this the following suggestions and hints will help you to organize and carry out this project.

SHED DORMER

1. Take a snapshot or make a sketch of your house and indicate where the dormer will go. Plan for a height of 7'6" and a length suitable for your attic project. Remember that a dormer should begin and end at a rafter.

2. Make a scale drawing of the dormer, showing every framing member in place. From this you can estimate the materials needed. Figure area of walls and roof to be covered by 1x8 sheathing and add about 20% for scrap.

3. First cut along the inside of the rafters down to the top plate on which the rafters rest. Start your cuts in a drilled hole and use a keyhole saw. The sawed boards are knocked loose from inside the attic.

4. Doubled corner studs are set up first and nailed to both top plate and to rafters which will later be cut. Check carefully with carpenter's level to make sure studs are vertical.

5. Frame the windows with double 2x4's set on edge across the top and a single 2x4 flat on the bottom. Six 10d nails are used to toenail each stud to plate. At this point your win-

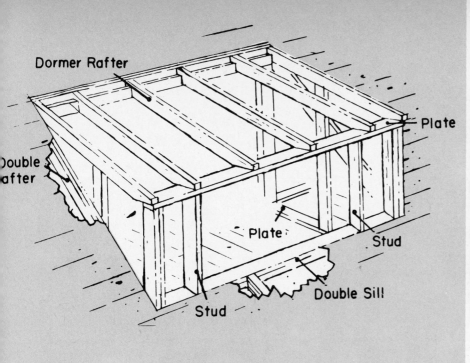

Dormer Rafter

Double Rafter

Plate

Plate

Stud

Stud

Double Sill

This shed dormer extends across the back of the house.

113

Planned for easy maintenance, this finished attic room for two young teen boys
leaves nothing to be desired. Floors are
covered with washable Armstrong Corlon,
and walls are finished in flat enamel. This
open plan, without confining walls, adds
spaciousness as no other plan can.

114

dow opening will depend upon the
style and amount of windows you
plan for the dormer.

6. Nail 1x6 blocks on opposing
rafters to support 16 foot 2x6 stringers. Toe-nail stringers to new top
plate with 8d nails.

7. Across the top edge of the new
opening nail a 1x6. Set rafters in
place and toe-nail with 8d nails to
the 1x6 at the top end, and to the
stringers at the other end.

8. After the new rafters are set in
their proper positions, the old ones
should be cut flush with the new studs
and the stringers. Then remove the
old ones. Nail 2x6's between stringers onto plates.

9. Starting at the front edge of the
roof, put roof sheathing across the
rafters.

10. Use 15# felt to cover the roof.
Carry the first strip down over the
stringer ends to underside. Cover the
underside of the dormer roof with
¼″ exterior grade plywood. Nail a
1x6 fascia board across.

11. Cover the felt with roll roofing,
starting at the fascia. The overlap of
strips is 2″ and use roofing adhesive
along seams and to coat the nail
heads.

12. Cut metal flashings and insert
6″ under old roofing and 8″ out over
last strip of new roofing. Coat this
flashing liberally with roofing compound along the edges.

13. Use 1x8 sheathing for front
and side walls. Cut the board ends
at the angle of the roof pitch to fit
flush against the roof.

14. The side sheathing is covered
with felt, starting at the bottom and

Photos courtesy Armstrong Cork. Co.
For the younger set, the campsite atmosphere so artfully generated will keep kids happy. The trees are real. They are cut to length and wedged in place. Note work-study area at far right.

overlapping 4″ over roof in front and at the sides.

15. Stock window frames are toe-nailed into the openings provided for them. Use your carpenter's level to make sure you have them in the proper position.

16. Metal flashing is run 6″ up the side and front walls and 4″ over roof all around. The siding is butted against the window casing. Rest the siding on the flashing.

17. Blanket insulation is applied between ceiling joists and between outer wall studs. Staple insulation back from front of studs to provide dead air space.

18. Finish the interior the same as the rest of the attic.

19. The exterior is finished with sheathing, shingles or other material to match the rest of the house.

Interior construction details are explained in this section on attics. Individual projects such as plumbing, wiring, and heating are explained in the sections under appropriate subject headings.

Awnings

The life of awnings may be prolonged with periodic inspection, care, and proper storage. Inspect the awnings when they are taken down in the fall, make all repairs necessary, so that next spring when they are again needed they will be in good condition.

Cleaning

Just before taking down, while awnings are still on the window, re-

115

Photos courtesy of National Cotton Council

Canvas panels, laced on metal frames made of aluminum tubing or pipe, are supported by upright pipes anchored to the concrete patio and secured to the edge of the roof. Used as a patio roof and as vertical shields to an overhang, the awnings give this contemporary home a bright new look.

move all dust with a stiff dry brush. Then dip the brush in a solution of lukewarm water and mild soap suds, and wash the awning. Remove soap suds with a clean cloth wrung out in clear lukewarm water. Let awnings remain open until thoroughly dry. Then take them down.

Repairing

If there are any frayed cords they should be replaced now. If the metal framework or the pulleys are rusted, or don't work easily, now is the time to remove the rust, to paint the framework, and oil the pulleys.

Any holes in the awning should be patched now. Use a rubber cement or other special glue which is obtainable at the hardware store, and attach the patch with this adhesive on the outside of the awning. Be sure to cut the patch about an inch bigger than the hole all around.

Painting

Use canvas paint. Hang the awning on the lowest window of your house; let the awning down, and paint it with long, even strokes. Do the entire job at once; if you try to do it in two days there might be streaks where you left off the first day. If your awning is striped, choose a paint to match the darker color of the stripe. The awning must remain opened until the paint is thoroughly dry.

Storing

The awning must be cleaned and repaired before it is packed away for the cold weather. It must be thoroughly dry, to prevent any danger of mildew. Fold the awning, cover it with heavy wrapping paper or a piece of canvas, and store it in a dry spot. If it needs painting, it is best to wait until you unwrap it next spring, and do the job at that time.

How to Make a Fixed Awning

You can keep Old Sol from beating through the windows in the summer and make your home a much cooler place in which to live. Permanent awnings not only are attractive but they have a cooling function as well.

Each awning should have a simple framework of 1 x 2 dressed lumber with cross-pieces 16″ apart. It should be covered with building panel that will last as long as the house. Masonite's Tempered Presdwood, either ¼″ or ³⁄₁₆″, will do that job. The panels may form a solid cover over the framework, or they may be cut into strips 4″ to 6″ wide and nailed to the framework with small spaces, about ¼″ to ³⁄₈″, between each strip.

If strips are used, use pieces of tempered hardboard of the same width under the framing too, spacing them to cover the openings above in the slanting portion of the awning.

If the solid-type covering is used, provide a couple of vent slots at the top of the awning to permit the escape of heated air.

Finish the awning with a good primer and two finish coats of a quality exterior type of paint. Use of different colors on alternating strips of the awning will produce a pleasing effect.

Awnings of this type will keep the inside temperature of your home from 5 to 10 degrees cooler on a scorching day.

Canvas Awning Projects

Cotton canvas, traditionally used for awnings, can help you live with the hot summer sun and like it. With this heavy fabric at your windows and doorways, your rooms will remain cool and comfortable despite high thermometer readings.

To stay on friendly terms with Old Sol, you need effective and flexible protection on all sides of your home.

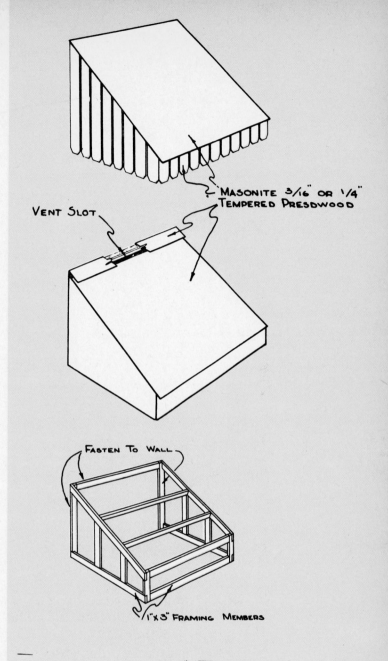

MASONITE ³⁄₁₆″ OR ¼″ TEMPERED PRESDWOOD

VENT SLOT

FASTEN TO WALL

1″ x 3″ FRAMING MEMBERS

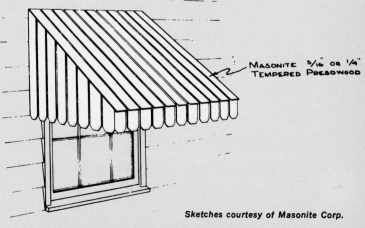

MASONITE ³⁄₁₆″ OR ¼″ TEMPERED PRESDWOOD

Sketches courtesy of Masonite Corp.

Here's one way to keep the sun from being an unwelcome house guest in the summer. Outside draw draperies keep the sun in its place when necessary but open the way for enjoyable indoor-outdoor living at other times of the day. They are hung on a conventional draw-drape rod, but make certain the hardware is rustproof.

In addition to overheating your rooms, the summer sun is likely to damage colors in your draperies, rugs and fabric-covered couches and chairs.

Whether you have standard or floor-to-ceiling windows, canvas awnings can be designed to solve your particular sun problems. They will keep indoor temperatures down and interior furnishings fresh and unfaded by effectively screening 75% of the solar rays. As soon as the sun changes its course or sets in the evening, cotton canvas awnings can be raised to let cool air enter your rooms.

Even if your house is air conditioned, your windows need to be protected from the sun. Recent studies show that glass lets in 35 times as much solar heat as an insulated wall. By intercepting the sun's rays, canvas awnings will reduce the cooling load on your air conditioning units and save money on their operation.

If you're tired of that closed-in feeling, use canvas to expand your home for modern summer living. With a window wall and connecting

Translucent plastic panels over a wood framework keep out glare but admit light to this pleasant patio.

Courtesy Filon Div., Vistron Corp.

terrace, you can double the space and livability of a room and open the way to pleasant outdoor entertaining and relaxing. A wide sweep of colorful canvas over the terrace will shade both indoor and outdoor areas.

If you have a window wall and no terrace, outside draw draperies of canvas will give you protection and privacy at a moment's notice. They will keep the sun in its place when necessary and allow you to invite nature indoors at other times of the day.

Canvas panels laced on metal frames and hinged to an overhang can contribute to your summer comfort in two ways. The panels may be extended horizontally as a patio roof

Pivot sun screens are practically a copy of the Venetian blinds you might have on your windows. It's easier to make these metal frames out of Do-It-Yourself Aluminum, but the more advanced handyman can try to do this with pipe. A tight fit into the flanges in the roof and floor will keep the sun screens moving in the breeze.

Photo and sketches courtesy of National Cotton Council

Old Sol traveling through the sky may strike at this western exposure in the late afternoon. But you won't have to worry about that if you have a vertical roller awning teamed with a wide roof overhang. The awning can be mounted on a shade roller or worked on a pulley system so that it moves up and down freely.

Sketches courtesy of National Cotton Council

This attractive overhang awning to shade the windows of the house and protect the walk in rainy weather, can be made by lacing canvas awning to a rigid iron or aluminum frame. The uprights are set into the ground, preferably into concrete, 8″ in diameter and about 12″ deep.

or dropped to hang vertically in front of your windows. A movable roof operated by pulleys will provide a shady spot by day and a cool open area by night.

Your awnings can be flattering additions to your house. You will find canvas in a myriad of gay solid hues and rainbow stripes. To rigid glass and wood or stone sidings, the heavy cotton fabric offers a bright and texturally-interesting contrast.

120

Like colored frosting on a cake, canvas can be the final decorative touch enhancing the eye-appeal of your house. A wise color choice will complement other elements making up the exterior. You may want to repeat the hue of your roof or match your sun shades to painted shutters and doors. Whatever color recipe you use, canvas will mix well with the other ingredients.

You can't change the weather outdoors but you can do something about your own private climate inside and surrounding your home. Canvas at your windows and doorways, and over your patio or terrace, can help you enjoy a cooler and happier summer. Awnings of this versatile fabric will not only protect your home from the sun's glare but give it new beauty.

Band Saw

The blade of this power saw consists of an endless, flexible steel band, with teeth cut on one edge. It revolves about two vertical pulleys or wheels, and is inserted through a hole in the horizontal table on which the cutting is done. The band saw is used for cutting curved edges or combinations of straight and curved work. Many

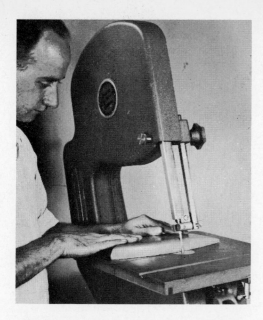

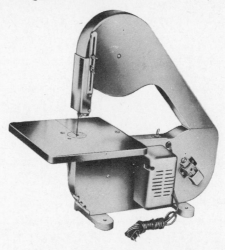

This band saw features a tilting mechanism permitting the handyman to do angle cutting. Note clamp guide and saw blade guard which protects the handyman when using the band saw.

Compact three-wheel band saw capable of cutting thin plywood to heavy 2x4's. The under blade capacity (below the blade and clamp guides) is 3¼". Comes with blower-cooled, built-in motor so that there's no need for pulleys or belts.

saws have a table that can be tilted 45° making bevel cuts possible.

The size of a band saw is measured by the diameter of the wheel; thus a saw with 10″ wheels would be called a 10″ saw. It can be mounted on a steel stand or wood bench, with the saw table about 43″ from the floor. For the home handyman a ⅓ H.P. motor will be strong enough. It should be a constant-speed, 1725 r.p.m. motor.

The operation of a band saw is relatively safe and simple and even an amateur can turn out a creditable piece of work. The most important precaution is to keep the blade sharp, since a dull blade requires greater feeding pressure with more tendency for the hand to slip.

Also see *SAWS*.

Banisters

Aside from the safety factor of a banister along the stairway, it should also be attractive and fit in with the decorating scheme of your house. If you feel that the existing banister is out-dated, replace it by building or buying one of more modern design.

In an enclosed stairway, or one leading to the basement or attic, there may be no banister or handrail. You could easily remedy the omission by a rope extended the full length of the stairway. Fasten to the wall either wooden or metal rings, spaced about three feet apart. Pull the rope through these rings and it acts as a handrail. The rope should be thick and smooth (no splintering). To make it more decorative, paint the rope (using a canvas paint) to match or contrast with the wall; or you might even sew a "slipcover" of a sturdy material to slide over the rope.

Also see *STAIRS*.

121

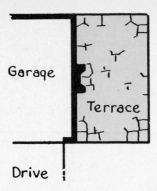

1. You can build your barbecue so that it is against the wall of your garage. However, provide a high chimney to keep the smoke away from your terrace or patio.

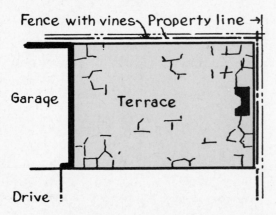

2. The barbecue can be built at one end of a terrace on a narrow lot. This will provide you with sufficient seating room away from the fire when the weather is too hot.

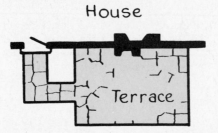

3. If your fireplace chimney in the house has a large enough flue or space for an added flue, you can build your outdoor fireplace up against the same wall and have it use the same chimney as your interior fireplace. But better check the flue to see if it can handle both before you start working on this project.

122

Barbecue

The outdoor fireplace is popularly referred to as the "barbecue." An outdoor fireplace and picnic area are now part of many home grounds as they provide entertainment and recreation for the family and their friends.

In planning a picnic area, the location of the fireplace, with its picnic furnishings, and the design and construction, are most important. Some fireplaces are elaborate and therefore costly; but these are not necessarily the best unless the surroundings demand one of intricate design. A simple low-cost fireplace can be fitted into a carefully planned scheme.

Location of Fireplace

The possible locations for a fireplace vary with the property on which it is to be constructed. It may be near the house or the garage or at some more distant place. A fireplace may be built onto the outside of a house chimney. Its flue should have a damp-

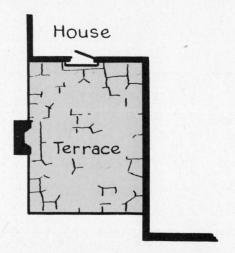

4. Here's another variation for building an outdoor fireplace. It can be built parallel with a house wall forming an attractive sitting area on the rectangular terrace.

er or be plugged in winter to prevent any interference with the draft in the flue of the home heating plant. The barbecue should not be near a frame building because of the fire hazard. Any local fire regulations must be observed. If the house is of stone, brick, or asbestos-shingle siding, the fire-hazard is not so great.

An outdoor fireplace near the house is convenient for carrying food and utensils from the house.

In more informal developments and where more space is available, the fireplace should have an adequate background of foliage. A fireplace without a chimney should face the prevailing winds so the smoke will be blown away from the cook and the table. A shade tree at the west or southwest of the picnic area provides shade for the table and chairs.

If the slope of the ground in front of the fireplace is such that furniture cannot be comfortably used, some grading and construction should be done.

Provide a level area for the furni-

5. If you want to keep the cooking away from your home and you have a large lot, build that barbecue in a corner near the property line.

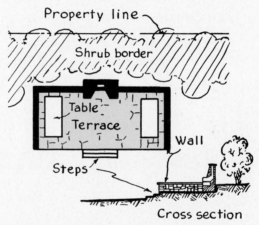

6. If your property slopes, it's better to build the barbecue on the higher ground than at the lower level. You will encounter less difficulty with smoke in this way.

123

7. Spacious outdoor living is yours on a large lot. Build your patio and the barbecue as its central focal point on the corner of your property. You can have your privacy by planting large shrubs on both sides facing your neighbors.

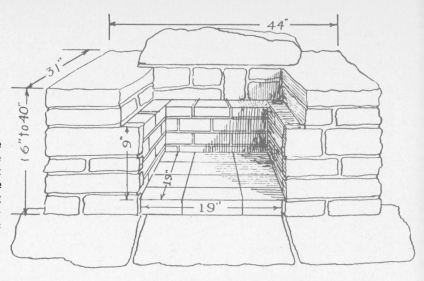

8. Details of a wood-burning fireplace made of stones and firebrick, used at the base. The amateur handyman should not attempt to build a stone barbecue until he has had sufficient experience in working with concrete and stone. See related masonry sections in these volumes for basic how-to.

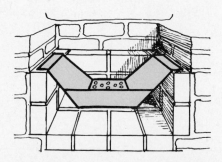

9. A shelf, or grate, can be used if you want to use charcoal in a wood-burning fireplace. You can purchase these grates in some hardware stores or make one out of sheet metal. Remove it during the winter or else it will rust and you'll have to buy a new one for next summer.

ture, and make enclosing walls high enough, about 16″ to 20″ above the floor of the terrace, to be used as seats at the table. The fireplace may be put in a natural grove of trees.

Fire Hazard

The fire hazard is not great, particularly if near-by buildings are fireproof or if the barbecue is about 50′ from the nearest building. One sel-

dom builds a roaring fire, for a fire burned down to coals provides the best cooking heat. Wood that crackles and snaps should not be used. A charcoal fire is excellent. Someone usually is near-by all the time the fire is burning and quick action can be taken in any emergency. The fire usually burns out of its own accord before the meal is over or soon after, but before leaving be sure that it is completely out.

Construction Material

Barbecues may be made of brick or stone or a combination of both. It is more difficult to obtain good results with round field stone than with flat stones, such as limestone. The firebox should be made of firebrick or of a highly glazed brick, because most types of stone crack or "explode" if submitted to intense heat. The foundation is made of concrete: 1 part of cement, 2 parts of sand, and 3 parts of gravel. A small fireplace with or without a chimney needs only a concrete slab from 4″ to 6″ thick and reinforced with old wire or metal rods. A larger fireplace, especially one with a chimney attached to a building, should have a foundation that extends about 42″ below the soil level or below the frost line. One sack of cement, 2 cubic feet of sand, and 3 cubic feet of gravel, will make about 3 to 3½ cubic feet of concrete. Three parts of sand and one part of cement are mixed into a mortar and used for the walls and the firebox.

Special metal grates are sometimes used, but adequate parts may be made from old pipes or metal sheets. The top section of an old wood or coal-burning kitchen range could be used. This assembly sometimes includes a reservoir for heating water.

Construction Plans

None of the plans shown need be followed exactly. The drawings merely illustrate the different types of outdoor fireplaces. Materials that are in harmony with the surroundings and those most conveniently available should be used.

A wood-burning fireplace usually has a firebox about 19″ square and 9″ high; the height and depth should not vary much from these dimensions. The length of the firebox and the outside dimensions can vary with the size of the available grates and according to your own desire. The shelves on each side of the grate should be large enough to set dishes and food near the cooking surface. The firebox is built first and then the shelf space.

Charcoal makes the best fire for cooking. A charcoal shelf or grate may be bent to fit a wood-burning fireplace. This can be made from a sheet of metal (28″ by 18″ for a 19-inch square firebox). Light-weight metal can be supported from underneath with bricks to prevent warping or bending. The depth of this adaptor, or grate, should be about 5″, and the sides should slope as shown. The bottom level is about 8″ wide. With the sloping sides and shallow depth, this conserves fuel and gives a good cooking heat. The front edge should have a low siding to keep the coals from falling on the hearth.

When charcoal only is used for fuel, it is better to build a fireplace for this purpose. The distance from the fine-mesh grate on which the charcoal is placed to the cooking grate above should be about 5″. Both grates may be larger than indicated if a larger cooking surface is desired. The grate should be closer to the front than to the back, so it will be easy to reach the cooking surface.

An elaborate fireplace with a chimney may include not only a wood storage box but warming ovens, grills, places to store outdoor furniture and many other special features that add to its usefulness. Shelves on the chimney are convenient for salt-and-pepper shakers, cooking spoons, forks, and small pans.

Unless large fires are built, the chimney need not be lined with flue tile. Such lining, however, is desirable as most stones and soft brick crack when subjected to sudden intense heat.

The floor of the wood box should slope, so water cannot stand and keep the wood wet.

125

LARGE BARBECUE

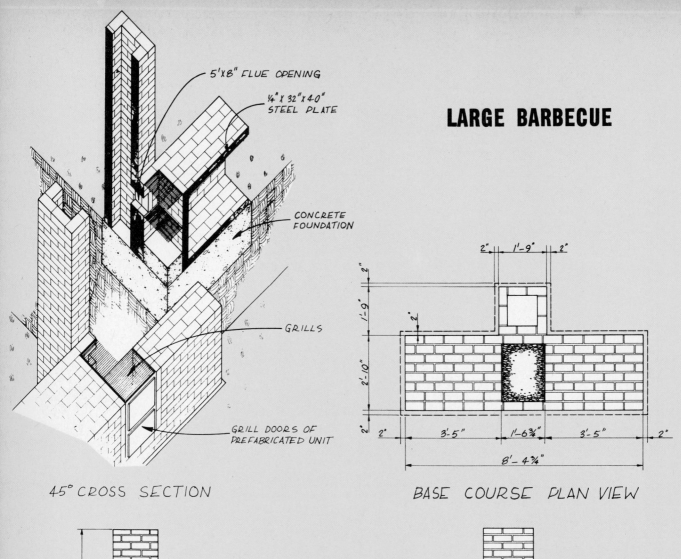

5'x8" FLUE OPENING

¼"x 32"x 40" STEEL PLATE

CONCRETE FOUNDATION

GRILLS

GRILL DOORS OF PREFABRICATED UNIT

45° CROSS SECTION

BASE COURSE PLAN VIEW

2"   1'-9"   2"

1'-9"

2'-10"

2"

2"   3'-5"   1'-6¾"   3'-5"   2"

8'-4¾"

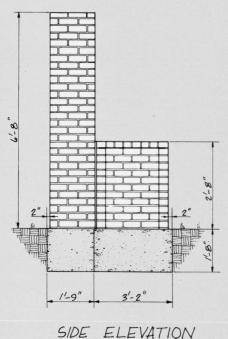

6'-8"

2'-8"

2"   2"

1'-8"

1'-9"   3'-2"

SIDE ELEVATION

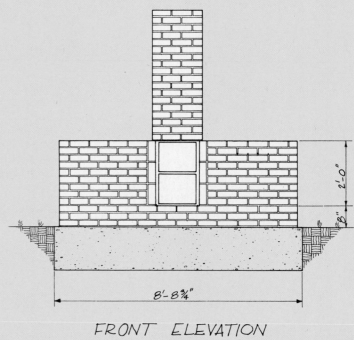

2'-0"

8"

8'-8¾"

FRONT ELEVATION

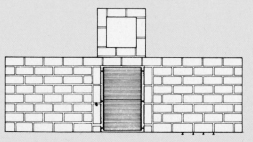

5" X 8" OPENING

1'-6¾"

CHARCOAL GRILL COURSE
PLAN VIEW

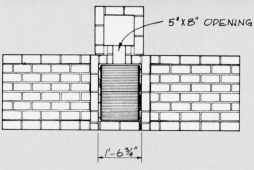

COOKING GRILL COURSE
PLAN VIEW

This large grill has storage areas at each end and two topside work surfaces. It can be built for about $75 (not including grill unit or battery-operated rotisserie).

MATERIAL LIST

ITEM	SIZE	QUANTITY
brick units	3¾" x 2¼" x 8"	684
steel plates	¼" x 2'8" x 3'4"	2
For Mortar:		
portland cement		2½ bags
hydrated lime		⅝ bag
loose, damp sand		7½ cu. ft.
For Concrete:*		
portland cement		15½ bags
loose, damp sand		30⅓ cu. ft.
crushed stone		37¾ cu. ft.

* Before mixing concrete for the foundation, set aside these materials for the hearth slab: 48 lbs. cement, 86 lbs. sand, 129 lbs. crushed stone.

BARBECUE

SMALL BARBECUE

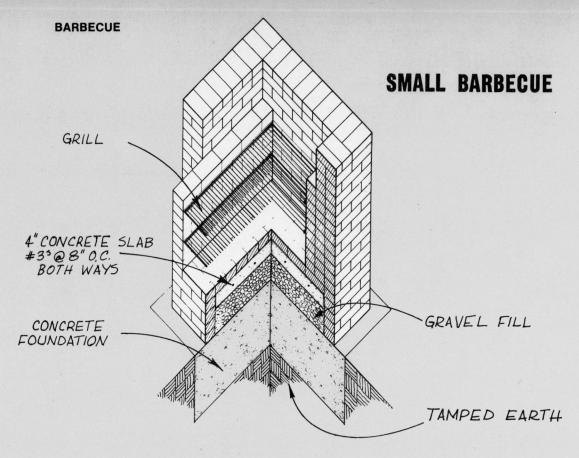

GRILL

4" CONCRETE SLAB
#3's @ 8" O.C.
BOTH WAYS

CONCRETE
FOUNDATION

GRAVEL FILL

TAMPED EARTH

45° CROSS SECTION

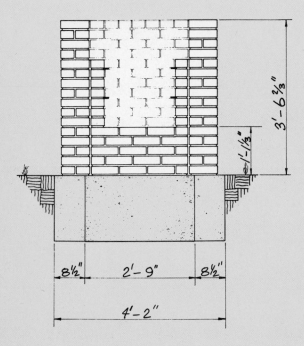

3'-6⅔"

1'-1⅓"

8½"   2'-9"   8½"

4'-2"

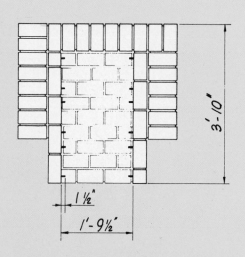

3'-10"

1½"

1'-9½"

PLAN VIEW
TOP COURSE and HEARTH

FRONT ELEVATION

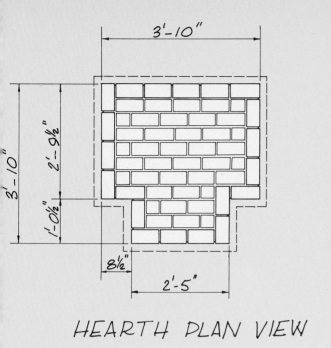

HEARTH PLAN VIEW

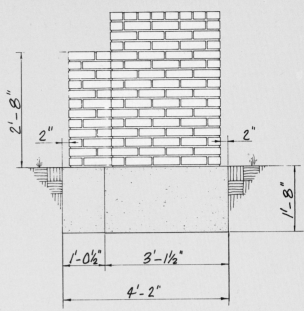

SIDE ELEVATION

This compact barbecue boasts a large cooking area, and its double-U design, with a double layer of bricks on the outside, provides a small work surface. Materials (not including grates) cost only about $35.

MATERIAL LIST

ITEM	SIZE	QUANTITY
brick units	3¾" x 2¼" x 8"	525
reinforcing steel	⅜"	22'
For Mortar:		2 bags
portland cement		½ bag
hydrated lime		6 cu. ft.
loose, damp sand		
For Concrete:*		8⅝ bags
portland cement		16¾ cu. ft.
loose, damp sand		21 cu. ft.
crushed stone		

* Before mixing concrete for the foundation, set aside these materials for the hearth slab: 40 lbs. cement, 72 lbs. sand, 109 lbs. crushed stone.

Photographs courtesy of Majestic Co., Inc.

1. Using stakes, mark out the area to be covered by your barbecue. Dig out this area to a depth of 12″. Now fill this opening to within 2″ of the top with gravel or crushed stone. Using 2x4 lumber, nail a form together so that it extends 2″ above the ground level along the perimeter of the opening.

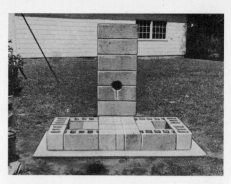

4. The wings for the barbecue are formed by setting a series of concrete blocks along the perimeter of the base. Use the 1:3 cement mix to hold blocks to base and to each other. Work carefully and make neat joints, using a pointed trowel or a short piece of pipe to produce a finished joint.

Easy-to-Build Barbecue

This deluxe barbecue is easily made by any handyman, even those who have never "buttered" a concrete block before. The total time is just two Saturdays: one to prepare and pour the base and the next (allowing time for the concrete base to harden) to erect the structure. Actually, it takes only two days to build this unit, but since curing of concrete cannot be rushed by the handyman, it's best to spread this job out over two weekends.

2. Mix a batch of concrete—1 part Portland cement, 2½ parts clean sand and 5 parts gravel, plus water. Pour 2″ of concrete, until level with the ground and then spread some heavy wire or hardware cloth across the opening. Now add 2″ more of concrete and level it smooth with top of form.

130

3. Use pre-formed 17″x21″ concrete chimney blocks (available in masonry supply yards) and set one atop the other with a mix of 1 part Portland cement to 3 parts sand, plus water. Use regular cement blocks, on their side, as the base for the grill; these are cemented together.

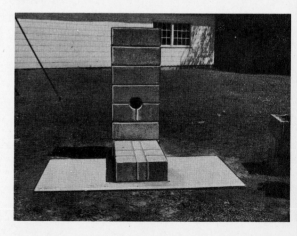

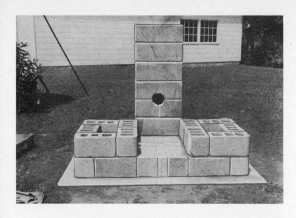

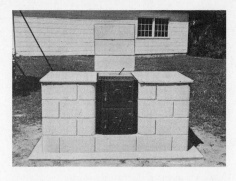

5. Since the grill unit will go in the center, build up both wings or sides by adding staggered rows of blocks upon each lower row. If your grill is 19″ wide, use a 3″ wide concrete block as a filler in the grill section. If the grill is only 15″ wide, this 3″ filler block can be omitted.

6. After three rows have been added above the base row for the wings, set a pre-formed concrete slab on top of each wing as a counter top. Secure with a 1:3 cement mix. The metal grill unit can be slipped into place between the two wings with the top level with the concrete slabs.

Two can cook as happily as one on this unique unit—a barbecue beside a fire pit. You can build similar units by adapting the plans shown in this section.

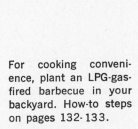

131

For cooking convenience, plant an LPG-gas-fired barbecue in your backyard. How-to steps on pages 132-133.

Outline base of barbecue with stakes, string.

Excavate and build a frame of 1x4 lumber.

Locate center and dig 24-inch hole for post.

Place post in hole and make sure it is plumb.

132

Pour concrete mix into frame; level and trowel.

Set forms for LPG tank, pour and level concrete.

Drive stakes into ground, nail frame to them.

Make sure that frame is level all around.

Fill hole with concrete and trowel surface.

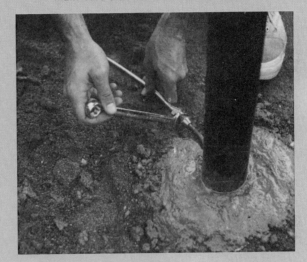

Attach gas line, then cover with bed of sand.

Connect LPG tank and set on stand behind unit.

Barbecue hides gas tank behind adjacent planter.

133

Photos courtesy Sakrete

One-Hour Barbecue

Rustic barbecues are easy and quick to make. These two models are particularly appropriate if you have just moved into your home and want a barbecue but don't have the time to build an elaborate one. Maybe, once you make either of these, you'll like it so much that you'll forget about that dream model.

Either of these two one-hour barbecues is made with brick. You need not use new brick. If you have some old brick about or can buy it cheaply in your area, you'll find that the old brick will add a certain decorative charm to that rustic appearance.

The pit for these units is dug out of the ground itself. Dig a hole about 8″ to 12″ deep. The circular model should be about 36″ in diameter and the rectangular rustic barbecue should be about 36″ long and about. 20″ wide. In both, the outside border or perimeter is made of brick set in the ground so that one half of the brick extends above the earth's surface.

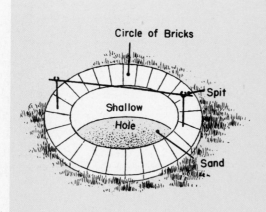

Dig a hole about 8″ to 12″ deep and about 36″ in diameter. Fill the bottom 4″ with sand or gravel and set the bricks around the outside edge so that one half of the brick extends above the earth's surface. A notched branch can hold the spit over the fire.

Another variation is the rectangular rustic model. This barbecue is about 20″ by 36″ and the bottom 4″ of the pit can be filled with sand or gravel. Use two spits, either home-made or store-bought.

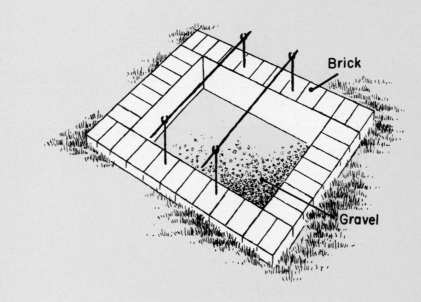

134

Circular Barbecue

You can have lots of fun with your family and friends sitting around a circular barbecue. Here's a very easy one to make. All you need is an old 55 gallon oil drum and some cistern blocks.

Cut the oil drum to one fourth of its original height. The shallow section serves as the fire base for the unit. You can set it flush on the ground. The outside walls are made of a double row of cistern blocks, set with or without mortar, on the ground level flush against the outside of the oil drum.

Grill-Warmer-Storage Unit

A few old bricks, some cement (either ready mixed or a 1:3 mix of Portland cement and sand) plus two iron grates are all you need to make this attractive barbecue. The center section is for the cooking of food. One side wing is for keeping the food warm over a small fire, while the other wing can be used for storage of wood.

This barbecue can be built directly on the ground. But if you live in an area of severe winters where the ground is apt to heave, dig down about 8″ and fill to within 1″ of the ground level with gravel and sand. Then build the unit on the top of this.

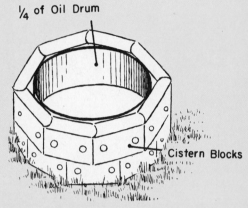

¼ of Oil Drum

Cistern Blocks

This inexpensive circular barbecue can be built by the handyman in just about an hour. If you cannot get an old 55 gallon oil drum, any large metal cån, over 20″ in diameter, will do. If you have small children about, use cement to hold the cistern blocks in place.

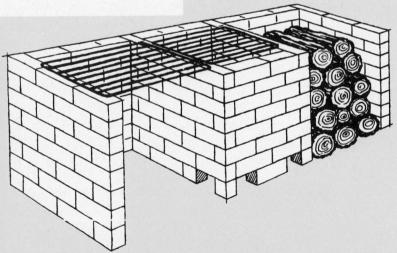

This combination barbecue can be built by the handyman in just a few hours. Leave two bricks out of the bottom row of the center unit to create the necessary draft for the fire. The iron grates are merely laid atop of the brick.

135

Built-in bar in this family room makes a congenial gathering spot, serving the adjacent patio as well.

Bars

136

A portable or built-in bar adds to the hospitality of the home when serving soft drinks for the teenagers or stronger beverages for the adult guests. The most appropriate place for the bar is in a recreation room, but it may also fit into the living or dining room, an alcove or foyer.

Converted Bars

A narrow table could easily be converted into a bar, by enclosing the front and two sides with plywood or wood boards, and leaving the back open. Build two shelves under the bar, of boards strong enough to carry the weight of glasses, bottles, and other necessary mixing apparatus. Paint or varnish the front and sides of the bar, and put a special liquid-proof finish on the top. Or you could cement to the surface a piece of left-over floor linoleum or a heavy plastic tabletop covering.

Enclosed bookshelves, which have a back and two sides, may also be converted into a bar. Turn the back of the bookshelves to face into the room, and use the shelves for all the glassware and mixings. Make the top, which is now the serving counter, liquid-proof through lacquering, varnishing or covering with a suitable material.

If you do not have much space to accommodate a bar, it could be placed on casters (one at each of its four corners) and rolled out when company arrives, then rolled away into an out-of-the-way spot when not in use.

Constructing a Bar

The length of the bar depends on the area you have available. A corner of the room is usually the best place to install the bar. The counter should be about 44″ from the floor; this is a convenient height to "bend the merry elbow" if the guests stand at the bar, and it is also good when they sit on the stools which are set in front of the bar.

The counter width should be about 20 inches; if possible extend it an inch in front of the bar, and two inches over the back.

In building a bar, you could use up some second-hand lumber, or buy new wood or plywood. First build a framework of 2x4's of the height, width, and depth needed for the bar. Then cut the plywood or wood boards to fit the front and sides of the bar, and nail these to the framework. Cut two shelves to fit under the bar, and nail them in. Last, the counter top is cut, and fastened down over the completed bar. For the shelves and top use a hard wood to accommodate weight.

Finish the outside of the bar with paint or varnish; the counter top to be lacquered, varnished or plastic laminated.

Making a Curved Bar

Add zest to the season's out-of-door parties by serving from a portable snack bar. You can make this unit to fit inside your home as well. Everything can be served from a snack bar with a two-tone curved front covered with a decorative material such as Masonite Leatherwood.

The bar should be 44″ high, 48″ across the back and have a 20″ radius. The top and bottom are cut out of ½″ plywood to shape shown in sketch with 1x2's cut for vertical supports. Space these about 6″ to 9″ apart along the circumference of the curved edge. Cut the Leatherwood panel to size and glue and nail in place. Add 3 casters to the bottom for easy moving.

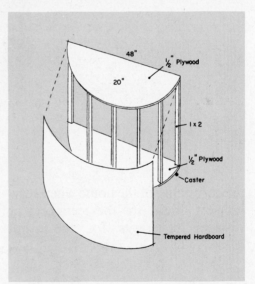

Details of the circular bar—top and bottom are cut out of ½″ plywood and vertical supports out of 1x2's. Secure plywood to supports with glue and two flathead screws, 1½″ long at each support. Countersink the screw heads. The ornamental face is glued and nailed to the plywood edges and the vertical supports. Casters are added to make the unit movable.

137

You can build one of these units, or all three to make a bar almost 6' long. You can install it against a wall or have it an island unto itself. Both left and right units have fold-back tops concealing racks that each store 20 bottles of wine. Underneath the rack of left unit is a compact refrigerator. The right unit has two slide-out bins, each with three shelves to store a large quantity of glasses. The center unit boasts a standard-size sink with a deep rollout bin for liquor and accessory storage.

Material List

• Lumber

Three 4'x8' sheets of ¾" DFPA rough-sawn plywood **(Note: If texture is desired on both sides, purchase 4'x8' sheets of ⅜" DFPA rough-sawn plywood and glue pairs of sheets together back-to-back before cutting.);** one 4'x4' sheet ¾" DFPA A-A plywood; one 4'x8' sheet ½" DFPA A-A plywood; one 2½'x8' sheet of plastic laminate veneer; 48' of ¾" x1" batten; 24' of ½" wood dowel; 5' of 5/16" wood dowel; 6" of ¾" wood dowel; 10"x22⅜"x1" hardwood cutting board.

• Hardware

Four 1½"x20½" piano hinges, ¾" screws as needed; three sets of 22" drawer slides (Knape and Vogt #1300); two pairs of cabinet hinges; two friction or magnetic catches; two lid stops (Stanley #435); one pound of 4d finishing nails; one pound of 3d finishing nails; white glue; eight 1½" #9 flat head wood screws; sixteen 1¼" #9 flat head wood screws; bar sink; plumbing supplies as needed; compact refrigerator; finishing materials (Thompson Water Sealer used on outside of unit shown).

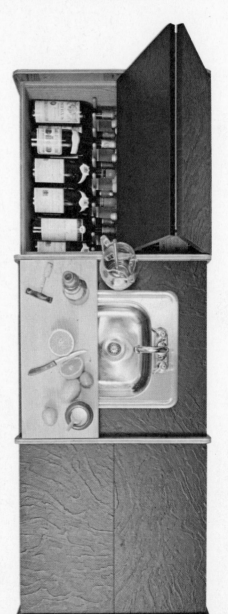

139

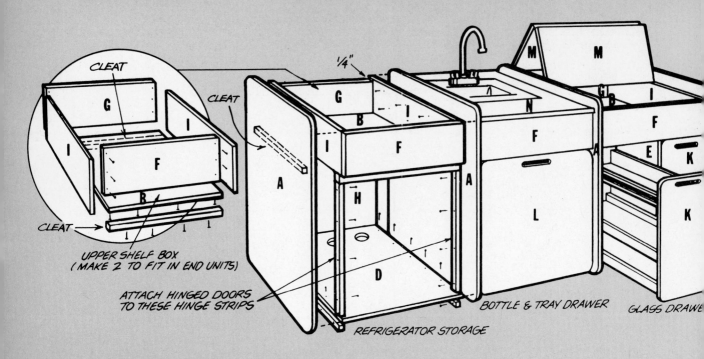

CLEAT

CLEAT

G

I

F

B

CLEAT

UPPER SHELF BOX
(MAKE 2 TO FIT IN END UNITS)

ATTACH HINGED DOORS
TO THESE HINGE STRIPS

1/4"

G

B

I

I

A

F

H

D

REFRIGERATOR STORAGE

M

M

N

F

L

A

G B

I

F

E

A

K

K

BOTTLE & TRAY DRAWER

GLASS DRAWER

1½" DIA AT ALL CORNERS
(CUT WITH SABRE OR COPING
SAW)

A

VERTICAL DIVIDER
(MAKE 4)

GRAIN

36"

26½"

UPPER SHELF
(MAKE 2)

B

21"

23½"

LOWER SHELF FOR
MIDDLE AND RIGHT
UNITS (MAKE 2)

C

23⅜"

22½"

2" DIA. VENT HOLES

LOWER SHELF FOR
LEFT UNIT (MAKE 1)

D

23⅜"

22½"

ALL PARTS SHOWN ARE
CUT FROM 3/4" ROUGH-
SAWN DFPA GRADE-
TRADEMARKED PLYWOOD.
TO ACHIEVE A TEXTURE
ON BOTH SIDES OF UP-

RIGHT DIVIDERS, GLUE
3/8" ROUGH-SAWN DFPA
GRADE-TRADEMARKED
PLYWOOD BACK TO
BACK — THEN CUT.

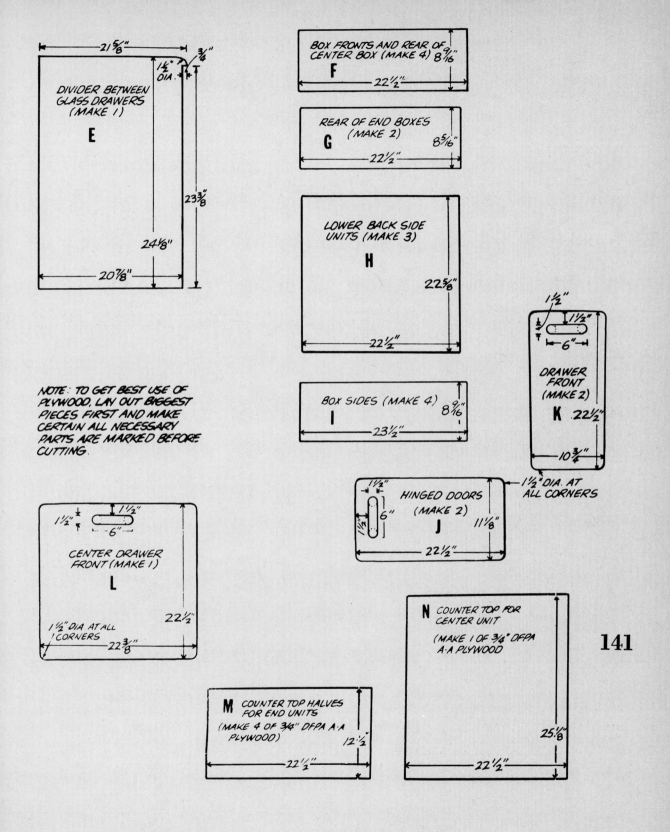

DIVIDER BETWEEN GLASS DRAWERS (MAKE 1) **E**
21 5/8"
3/4"
1 1/2" DIA.
23 3/8"
24 1/8"
20 7/8"

BOX FRONTS AND REAR OF CENTER BOX (MAKE 4) 8 9/16"
F
22 1/2"

REAR OF END BOXES (MAKE 2)
G
8 5/16"
22 1/2"

LOWER BACK SIDE UNITS (MAKE 3)
H
22 5/8"
22 1/2"

BOX SIDES (MAKE 4)
I
8 9/16"
23 1/2"

1 1/2"
1 1/2"
6"
DRAWER FRONT (MAKE 2)
K 22 1/2"
10 3/4"
1 1/2" DIA. AT ALL CORNERS

NOTE: TO GET BEST USE OF PLYWOOD, LAY OUT BIGGEST PIECES FIRST AND MAKE CERTAIN ALL NECESSARY PARTS ARE MARKED BEFORE CUTTING.

1 1/2"
6"
HINGED DOORS (MAKE 2)
J
11 1/8"
22 1/2"

1 1/2"
6"
CENTER DRAWER FRONT (MAKE 1)
L
22 1/2"
1 1/2" DIA. AT ALL CORNERS
22 3/8"

N COUNTER TOP FOR CENTER UNIT
(MAKE 1 OF 3/4" DFPA A·A PLYWOOD
25 1/8"
22 1/2"

M COUNTER TOP HALVES FOR END UNITS
(MAKE 4 OF 3/4" DFPA A·A PLYWOOD)
12 1/2"
22 1/2"

141

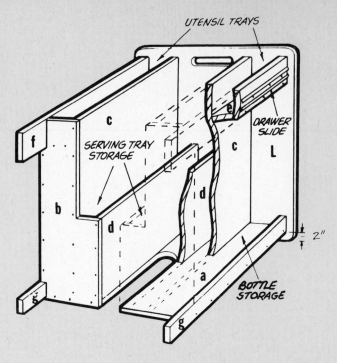

UTENSIL TRAYS

DRAWER SLIDE

c

f

SERVING TRAY STORAGE

b

d

c

L

d

a

BOTTLE STORAGE

2"

g

g

FIG. 2 CENTER DRAWER DETAIL

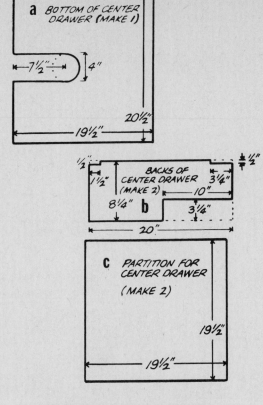

a BOTTOM OF CENTER DRAWER (MAKE 1)

7½"

4"

20½"

19½"

BACKS OF CENTER DRAWER (MAKE 2)

½"

½"

1½"

3¼"

10"

8¼"

b

3¼"

20"

c PARTITION FOR CENTER DRAWER (MAKE 2)

19½"

19½"

d PARTITION FOR CENTER DRAWER (MAKE 2)

9½"

19½"

e TRAYS FOR CENTER DRAWER (MAKE 2) 4½"

19½"

f

23"

3¾"

OUTER SIDE OF UPPER TRAYS IN CENTER DRAWER (MAKE 2)

g

23"

1½"

OUTER SIDE OF BOTTOM IN CENTER DRAWER (MAKE 2)

ALL PARTS SHOWN ARE CUT FROM ½" A·A INT·DFPA GRADE-TRADEMARKED PLYWOOD UNLESS OTHER-WISE NOTED.

NOTE: TO GET BEST USE OF PLYWOOD, LAY OUT BIGGEST PIECES FIRST AND MAKE CERTAIN ALL NECESSARY PARTS ARE MARKED BEFORE CUTTING.

142

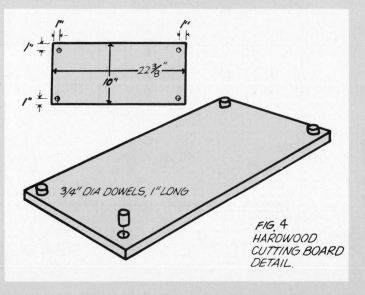

1"

1"

1"

22⅜"

10"

1"

3/4" DIA DOWELS, 1" LONG

FIG. 4 HARDWOOD CUTTING BOARD DETAIL.

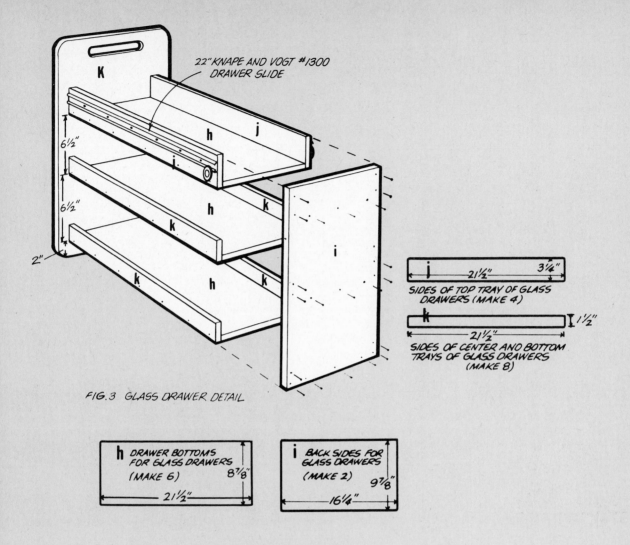

22" KNAPE AND VOGT #1300 DRAWER SLIDE

6½"

6½"

2"

K

h

j

i

h

k

k

h

k

j 21½" 3¾"

SIDES OF TOP TRAY OF GLASS DRAWERS (MAKE 4)

k 21½" 1½"

SIDES OF CENTER AND BOTTOM TRAYS OF GLASS DRAWERS (MAKE 8)

FIG.3 GLASS DRAWER DETAIL

h DRAWER BOTTOMS FOR GLASS DRAWERS (MAKE 6) 8⅞" 21½"

i BACK SIDES FOR GLASS DRAWERS (MAKE 2) 9⅞" 16¼"

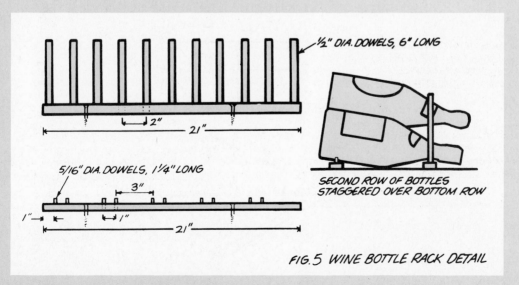

½" DIA. DOWELS, 6" LONG

2" 21"

5/16" DIA. DOWELS, 1¼" LONG

3"

1" 1" 21"

SECOND ROW OF BOTTLES STAGGERED OVER BOTTOM ROW

143

FIG.5 WINE BOTTLE RACK DETAIL

Plans For a Basic Bar

Maybe you'd like to stick to the traditional rectangular-shaped bar. Here is a simple, easy-to-make frame, which can be finished in a variety of ways to suit many tastes. Just follow the step-by-step plans noted in the accompanying illustrations.

A. Basic frame starts with a base cut out of 1x6 lumber with butt joint corners joined with three flathead screws each. A ½" plywood base is attached to the top of the 1x6 frame with screws or 4d common nails. The sides are made of 2x2 lumber with a center horizontal support to hold a shelf. The bar top is made of ½" plywood which is attached to the sides, which in turn are secured to the base plywood and frame. Notch out the corners of the ½" plywood shelf and set in place.

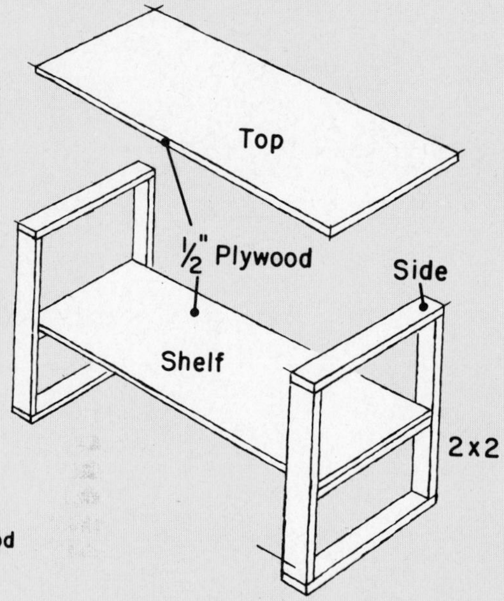

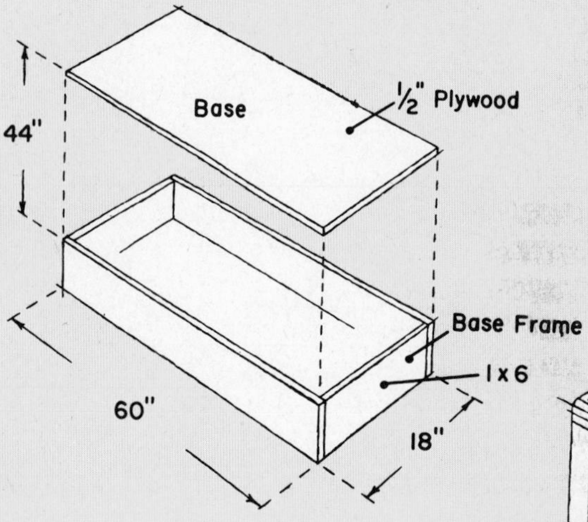

B. You can use the plywood as the finished top of the bar or you can attach durable, easily-washed laminated plastic with contact cement. A lip edge is often used; in this case a piece of ½" quarter-round or other decorative molding is cut with mitered corners to fit across the front and sides of the bar and secured with 4d finishing nails.

144